Zen Buddhism
The Pathway to Nirvana

Scott Shaw

Buddha Rose Publications

ISBN: 1-87777-9236-5
ISBN-13: 978-1877792366

First Edition 2007
Second Edition 2011

Library of Congress Control Number:
2008942167

10 9 8 7 6 5 4 3 2 1

Printed in the United States of America

Zen Buddhism
The Pathway to Nirvana

Table of Contents

Introduction

Zen Buddhism, the term conjures up images of robed individuals, with heads shaved, walking placidly through a garden like environment, consciously communing with nature.

Zen Buddhism, the term depicts a Master seated in lotus posture with his mind unswayable from the deep realms of meditation.

Zen Buddhism, the expression brings images to the mind of the simple, yet extremely beautiful paintings of ancient artists who portrayed the Asian landscape with the exacting detail, using only simple brush strokes.

Zen Buddhism describes meditation and solitude.

Zen Buddhism defines a road to Nirvana that has been portrayed as a distant plateau, obtainable only by the most holy.

But, Zen Buddhism is much more than all of this.

The foundations of Zen were laid centuries ago. The roots of Zen can be traced to the teaching of Siddhartha Guatama, the Sakyamuni Buddha, who lived and taught in India beginning in the fifth century Before the Common Era.

The essence of what was later to become Zen did not begin to become formalized, however, until the great Buddhist sage, Bodhidharma, traveled from his native India to become the abbot of the Shoshang (Shaolin) Monastery in China, in the fifth century of the Common Era. Though not the first to make this journey, he set in motion a pattern of understanding that would affect the evolution of Buddhist thought forever.

Bodhidharma emphasized the need for the Guru disciple relationship and the absolute necessity of meditation. From Bodhidharma was born a lineage of patriarchs who held the keys to enlightenment and passed this knowledge forward through exacting methods of formalized transmission.

As the centuries progressed, the evolution of Zen Buddhism was not always a placid pathway, however. In the seventh century of the Common Era, the Chinese schools of Zen began to split. The initial rift occurred when the fifth patriarch, Hung-jen awarded his disciple, Hui-neng with the seal of enlightenment. The other monks of the order became jealous and Hui-neng had to flee the countryside in fear of their reprisals. From this occurrence two distinct schools of Chinese Zen Buddhism were set in development. Though envy and jealously are hardly byproducts of Buddhism, this rift aided to the ongoing evolution of Zen Buddhist thought.

With these two distinct schools of Chinese Zen Buddhism as the impetus, new schools, with unique understandings of Buddhism, begin to evolve and come into existence throughout China.

As time progressed, Chinese Zen Buddhism was forced to overcome many obstacles, particularly political, as the dominated Chinese philosophic mindsets of Taoism and Confucianism were challenged by this evolving philosophy. By the time of the Chinese Song Dynasty (960-1279 CE.), however, Chinese Zen Buddhism had established itself as a viable pathway to cosmic consciousness and was accepted into the mainstream of Chinese philosophic and artistic thought.

From China, Buddhism was transmitted to the Korean peninsula, during the 4th century of the Common Era. From Korea it expanded to the island nation of Japan during the 5th century. As Buddhism came to be embraced and extend across Japan, its evolution was no more tranquil than it had been in China. Powerful Buddhist temples were substantiated. These temples held possession over large amount of farmland. The temple patriarchs would lease the land and collect large taxes for its usage. To enforce their land holdings, as well as to engage in expansionistic battles against other Monasteries, they employed Buddhist based Samurai warriors.

It was not until 1180 of the Common Era, when the Minamoto family took control over Japan in the Gempei War, that the warring factors gave way to the Kamakura Shogunate. With this, Royalty was displaced and the first wholly militaristic government came to power in Japan. From this unification, political Buddhism was put to rest, and the spiritual side of the philosophy was again allowed to flourish. This power structure ruled Japan until 1868.

During this time period, two individuals, who would later become defining elements in the evolution of Zen Buddhism, traveled from their native Japan to China in order to study Buddhism. The first was Eisai (1141-1215). The second was Dogen (1200-1253). Eisai studied the Linji tradition, which came to be known as the Rinzai School in Japan and Dogen studied from the Zaodong sect that became the Soto School. Upon returning to their native Japan these two teachers laid the foundations for what has become modern Zen Buddhism.

Whereas the Soto School founded by Dogen focused primarily upon meditation as the primary pathway to enlightenment, the Rinzai school of Eisai taught that an individual could also experience enlightenment by way of the Koan. The Koan is an abstract statement of words that causes the mind to be altered from the normal patterns of thought. Once the mind has shifted away from ordinary thinking, it is able to obtain a glimpse of absolute consciousness or enlightenment.

As the centuries have progressed, Japan has moved to the forefront of Zen Buddhism. Though various schools have splintered off from the original Rinzai and Soto traditions, the techniques of formalized Zen Buddhism have remained fairly constant, with meditation, a monastic lifestyle, and the practice of Koan contemplation at the heart of the teachings.

Though these pathways have become what are accepted as the traditional depiction of Zen Buddhism. Zen, itself, is much more than simply a tradition based in formalized contemplation and meditation. Zen is a pathway that utilizes the most abstract forms of paradox and contradiction to guide its practitioners towards the ultimate goal of enlightenment.

Beginning in the 1940's and more demonstratively during the 1950's and 1960's, Zen Buddhism began to impact the shores of the Western World. This occurred, hand-in-hand, with the counter-culture revolution that was taking place. The cosmic understanding of enlightenment, inherent to Zen, became one of the key mindsets that was embraced by this generation.

At this juncture, again, Zen Buddhism evolved from its formalized foundations, just as it had done an untold number of times in the past. With this, Zen Buddhism moved to its next plateau, where it was no longer required that the practitioner live a celibate, meditative lifestyle, locked within the wall of a monastery in order to find Nirvana. Instead, it came to be understood that everyone, even those with a job to go to, bills to pay, and a family to take of, could touch enlightenment.

As this new evolution of Zen Buddhism took place, there were many critics who claimed that only the established, formalized understanding of Zen Buddhism was the true pathway to enlightenment. But, these critical individuals forget the evolution of this philosophy and how with each passing age it has moved onto new realms of understanding, with new enlightened beings transcending the constrains of human limitations all the time.

At its heart, Zen Buddhism is a pathway to enlightenment. From Zen we learn that enlightenment is available to anyone who wishes to remove his or her mind from the controlling hands of the known and consciously move to a new level of abstract understanding. To this end, in the pages of this book Zen Buddhism and its techniques will be discussed as a method that can be understood and employed by everyone.

No longer is Nirvana only available to the monk sitting in a monastery. Nirvana is here. Nirvana is now. And, it can be experienced by anyone who has the mind to embrace this cosmic understanding.

PART I
Zen Buddhism: The Foundations

The essence of Zen Buddhism is based on the teachings of a man who has come to be known simply as, *"The Buddha."* The Sanskrit term, *"Buddha,"* means, *"One who has awakened."* This individual, who traveled and taught in India over two thousand years ago, has come to be thought of as one of the most all-knowing beings in human history. From his teachings the various sects of the Buddhist faith arose—ultimately culminating in the school of philosophic thought known as Zen Buddhism.

To understand Zen Buddhism, one must first come study the life and teaching of this historical figure. By understanding what he taught and how his teachings evolved throughout the centuries, a true understanding of Zen Buddhism can arise, providing the interested individual or practitioner with the foundational knowledge necessary to press forward into deeper understandings of Zen.

14

Chapter **1**

The Buddha

Historically, little is of absolute certainty regarding the life of the being who has become commonly referred to as the Buddha. Throughout history, however, his life has been chronicled in legend.

Siddhartha Guatama

Siddhartha Guatama, the Sakyamuni Buddha, _"Buddha from the Kingdom of Sakya,"_ is generally agreed to have lived from 563 to 483 BCE. Legend states that he was a Prince from the Kingdom of Sakya. This kingdom was geographically located in what is now modern-day Nepal. As a prince, he lived a very sheltered life. Upon witnessing poverty, illness, and death for the first time, he lost faith in all that was material and left behind his royal lifestyle in pursuit of the ultimate truth of human existence.

What is historically established is that during the life of the Buddha a revolution was taking place in South Asia. Iron had been introduced to the Indian Subcontinent from China. This led to rapid advancements in society. Agriculture was vastly improved and landscapes could be readily cultivated. No longer were the forests the daunting obstacles they had once been.

Now, they could be cleared so that crops could be harvested within their once impenetrable boundaries. New structures, particularly palaces, were constructed in a much more substantial fashion. And perhaps most definitive of the era, the tool of warfare were vastly improved. So much so, that near the end of his life, the Buddha's own kingdom of Sakya fell to the neighboring Kingdom of Kosala. Within a century of his lifetime, the entire region of what is now Northern India and Nepal would be united as the Magadha Empire.

The prominent religion of this historic era was Vedic Brahanism, which can most closely be compared to modern Hinduism. This religion can trace its roots back a thousand years prior to the life of the Buddha. Its scriptures, known as The Vedas, began to be composed in 1500 BCE.

The highest practitioners of this religion were, *"The Brahmans."* They were identified as the highest cast and obviously the wealthiest of this ancient society. From this, they claimed privileges not afforded to the average individual.

As formalized power, secular wealth, and religious privilege rose in this region, dissatisfaction among the populace also escalated. This gave birth to a group of ascetics who were known as, *"Sramana."* The Sramana shunned society, renounced material possessions, and became wandering holy men following an undefined path to enlightenment. This group laid the foundations for what has become more commonly known as the Sadhu. The mindset of this group, undoubtedly, influenced the path the young Siddhartha Guatama, as he would ultimately follow in this tradition.

The Buddha's path to enlightenment is historically unclear. It is believed that he studied with two primary teachers, Arada Kalama, who taught Akimcanya Ayatana, *"The experience of nothingness"* and, Udraka Ramaputra, who taught *"Naiva Samjna Asamjna Ayatana,"* *"The experience of conscious unconsciousness."*

The Enlightenment of The Buddha

Legend states that the Buddha, dissatisfied with not obtaining the ultimate understanding of life or enlightenment from his two teachers and tiring of following the path of a wandering holy man, sat down under a Bodhi Tree and swore he would not rise until he became enlightened. Though many legends have been written about what the Buddha experienced during this period of intensive meditation, it is known that he did, in fact, raise an enlightened being.

The Buddha, upon his realization, gave his first enlightened discourse at what is now Bodh Gaya, near Varanasi, India. This talk is defined as, *"The First Turning of the Wheel of Dharma."*

It cannot be established, with absolute certainly, what the Buddha actually said during this discourse or in subsequent discourses. All that is written, claiming him as the source, was done so years, and in some cases centuries, after his physical death.

The Pali Canon

The Theravada tradition of Buddhism claims that the language of the Buddha was Pali, and thus, their collections of scriptures, known as, *The Pali Canon,* is the most accurate. This, however, has proven to be linguistically incorrect, as Pali came into existence after the time of the Buddha—who left his body near the city of Kusinagra, when he was eighty years old.

Thus, his spoken words, though possibly initially recorded in his native dialect, most probably, Magadhi, were handed down from disciple to disciple for an undefined period before they finally found their way into scriptural form in The Pali Canon.

The Evolution of Buddhism

With the physical death of the Buddha, his disciples began to spread his teachings, initially through out India and then the world. With each new transmission of knowledge, the teachings of the Buddha began to be practiced in new and unique ways. From this, the various schools of Buddhist thought began to emerge, include Zen Buddhism.

Chapter 2
The Buddhist Religion

With the end of the Buddha's life came the Buddhist religion. But, it must be understood that the Buddha did not invent the concept of enlightenment, nor was he the first, or the last, being to reach this highest level of conscious evolution. Throughout the centuries the followers of Buddhism have come to idealize his life and his teachings to the degree that it has become impossible for most of them to reach their own Buddhahood. This is due to the extensive set of parameters they have assigned to the advancement of human consciousness.

There is an elemental problem with this mindset, however. Was the Buddha a Buddhist? No, he was not. Did the Buddha ask for worship? No, he did not. In fact, legend states that when he was asked, *"Are you a god,"* he answered, *"No, just a man."* When asked, *"Then, are you a Guru?"* He answered, *"No, just a man."*

This is the portrait of the true, perfectly enlightened teacher—one who has achieved the highest level of human consciousness and yet does not seek admiration due to his realization.

It is the unenlightened mind of humanity that has forgotten this simple truth and has chosen to make the Buddha a deity of worship and his teachings the basis for a religion. From this mindset has come centuries of Buddhists that have been unable to encounter the realms of Nirvana— solely due to the fact that they project such an orchestrated, idealized image of what enlightenment is supposed to be. This problem is amplified by the fact that many Buddhists hold fast to the belief that the teachings of their sect of Buddhism or the teachings of their individual teacher hold the only great truth and are the only pathway to achieve enlightenment. They miss the point...

The teachings attributed to the Buddha are absent from formalized religion. Formalized religion employs ritual. Ritual, though beautiful to watch, is based in physical actions. Physical actions only lead to physical reactions. Thus, Karma is set in motion, not enlightenment.

If enlightenment is the core teaching of the Buddha, and his teaching detail that it is possible for each individual to achieve this level of consciousness, then why does anyone do anything but become enlightened? Arguing that my school or my teacher is the best and yours is wrong does not produce enlightenment. It only produces conflict.

It is within this mindset of conflict, however, that the stage for the ongoing evolution of Buddhism was set in motion. The ongoing evolution of Buddhism eventually orchestrated the foundations of Zen Buddhism. Therefore, to come to understand how Zen Buddhism evolved from the teachings of the Buddha, the evolution of Buddhism must be studied.

The Four Councils of Buddhism

One month after the physical death of the Buddha in 463 BCE, a gathering of his disciples took place. This congregation was named, *"The First Council."* The First Council was held at Rajagha, India. This council was led by the most senior enlightened disciple of the Buddha, Mahakasyapa.

The First Council was organized in order to draw together the Buddha's disciple and to formulate an exact set of doctrine for the formulized teachings of the Buddha to move forward. At this council, the Dharma and the *Vinaya* where discussed. The Dharma is the pathway of the Buddha's teachings and the *Vinaya* is the code of conduct embraced by the disciples.

At this first council, all of, *"The Arhat," "Disciples of the Buddha, who had relinquished the ways of the world,"* came the conclusion that the teachings of the Buddha were prefect and that no changes should take place in either content or form. During this early period of Buddhism little conflict existed and the Arhat walked a very strict path of discipleship: practicing celibacy, rebuking all forms of desire, and emotions, and leading a very meditative lifestyle.

The Second Council

One hundred years after the passing of the Buddha, *"The Second Council"* was called. This council is believed to have taken place either in Patalipurta or Vaisali, in modern day India, in approximately 636 BCE. By this point in history differences of practice and spiritual ideologies had already begun to form within the Buddhist community. Though there was no controversy over the actual teachings of the Buddha, the Dharma, at this juncture, had fragmented and two distinct schools of Buddhism emerged: Sthavarivada and Mahasanghika.

The group of practitioners who came to be known as, *"The Sthavarivada,"* believed that the teachings of the Buddha and the practices he prescribed were perfectly formulated and that nothing should be changed. The group of practitioners that came to be known as, *"The Mahasanghika,"* were less convinced, however, about the absolute nature of the Buddha's teachings and began to follow a less regimented pathway to enlightenment. From these actions, the Sthavarivada began to consider the Mahasanghika lackadaisical practitioners.

Beginning with The Second Council the singular teachings of the Buddha began to fragment. From this, the first two distinct Schools of Buddhism came into existence.

Theravada

"The Third Council," was called together in 330 BCE. This council was held in Pattlipura, in what is modern day India.

This council was called during the reign of King Ashoka, who ruled over much of the India Subcontinent from 273 to 232 BCE. King Ashoka was a highly active convert to Buddhism. Thus, he accelerated the expansion of Buddhist thought throughout the India subcontinent.

The Buddhist leader of the second council was Moggaliputta Tissa. At the council he presented the text, "Kathavatthu." Kathavatthu, translates from Pali as, "Points of Controversy." This seven-volume canon was Moggaliputta Tissa's attempt to revitalize the structure of the Buddhist religion and define the faults that he felt existed within the Buddhist community. The revitalized teachings of Moggaliputta Tissa were accepted and this third council became known as, "The Council of the Theravada."

"Theravada," translates from Pali as, "The Teaching of the Elders." It is sometimes referred to as "The Lessor Vessel" or "Small Boat" school of Buddhism. This delineation has been a hotly debated topic over the centuries, but the terminology is used to imply the fact that the teachings of Theravada are based upon an individual's pathway to enlightenment, as opposed to a larger group consciousness moving towards this ultimate goal.

Theravada is the longest surviving school of Buddhist practice. As the centuries have progressed, Theravada is the primary school of Buddhist thought practiced in Southeast Asia and Sri Lanka. Theravada utilizes the teaching of, Vibhajyavada or *"Self-analysis,"* as its primary tool that guides the practitioner towards self-realization. What this style of Buddhism details is that the practitioner must analyze each element of him or herself and the teaching of the Buddha, thereby revealing the true, Buddha-nature.

Mahayana

"The Forth Council of Buddhism" was called in 100 CE. It was held in Jalandhar, in modern day Kashmir. This council is commonly referred to in the works of Theravada Buddhism as, *"The Council of the Heretic Monks."*

The Forth Council was convened under Emperor Kanishka. The Buddhist monk Vasumitra was the leader of the council. At this council it was decided that the Buddhist canons that had been composed up to this point needed to be reevaluated, annotated, and edited. It was this action that angered the traditional schools of Theravada Buddhism.

It was at this Forth Council where the tradition of Mahayana Buddhism was formally born. *"Mahayana,"* or the, *"Great Vehicle school of Buddhism,"* is the style of Buddhism which is predominately embraced in China, Korea, Japan.

Zen Buddhism falls under the lineage of Mahayana Buddhism.

Chapter 3
China and Buddhism

As faith in the Buddha and his teachings began to spread from its source in India, it traveled northward over the Tibetan plateau until it found its way to China where it began to slowly be embraced. This transmigration was not an easy pathway, however, as the native Shamanism of Tibet and the strongly held, highly defined, religious idealism of China had to be encountered.

The primary reason Buddhism finally came to find acceptance in China was due to the fact that when the teaching of the Buddha were being translated into Chinese, by India Buddhist monks, the words, terms, and the ideologies of the native Chinese philosophic school of thought of Taoism were used to convey the Buddhist ideologies. From this, many of the early Chinese followers of Buddhism actually believed it to be a subdivision of Taoism.

Whether the process of integrating Taoism into the teachings of the Buddha was a conscious or unconscious process may never be historically verified. None-the-less, what occurred is that Buddhism began to slowly spread across China where it was ultimately heartily embraced, giving birth to some of the most essential trends in the evolution of Buddhism.

The Chinese schools of Taoism played essential roles in the expansion of Buddhism. It was the Taoist love and revere for nature that truly gave rise to some of the most essential elements of Buddhism. For this reason, the religious history of China elementally helped to formulate many of the factors associated with Buddhism throughout the centuries.

Religious History in China

Religious history in China can be dated back to the Xia Dynasty, existing forward from approximately 2200 BCE. Historically little is known about this period of Chinese history. There are, however, archeological fragments of Oracle Bones suggesting that human religious sacrifices took place. In approximately 1600 BCE the Shang Dynasty developed in Northern China. The Shang Dynasty had a strict system of State Loyalty in association with reverence for village elders and priests of the dominant tribal religion. This belief system of duty to the government and devotion to the religious hierarchy has permeated the Chinese mindset from that period of Chinese history forward into modern times.

The Zhou Dynasty was formulated in 1027 BCE. This dynasty followed the overthrow of the Shang Dynasty. Between 771 and 770 BCE an uprising to the Zhou authority took place and dissidence within the Zhou nobility left the formal confines of the kingdom and allied themselves with nomadic tribes from the North. From this political disruption a period of social chaos occurred in China followed. It is known as the Warring States Period.

During the Warring States Period of Chinese history several of the most profound written works defining Chinese culture and philosophy were created. These texts include: *"The Tao Te Ching," "The Inner Chapters," "The Confucian Doctrines," "Sun Tzu: The Art of War,"* and *"Huang Ti Nei Ching Su Wen," "The Yellow Emperor's Classic of Internal Medicine."*

Taoism

One of the most influential schools of philosophic thought to emerge from China, especially in regard to the mystical arts, is that of Taoism. The Chinese term, *"Tao,"* is translated as, *"Way." "Way"* refers to the unceasing flow of energy in this universe and the path an individual walks until they ultimately merge and become a conscious part of this cosmic energy.

Taoism was formulated in the Chinese state of Ch'u in the Yangtze Valley. It initially developed in approximately 1000 BCE. It is believed that in its initial form, Taoism represents an enrichment of Chinese thought derived in part from, *"Barbarian sources."* The Barbarians, as they were referred to, were wandering nomads who lived outside the scope of the accepted Chinese governmental influence. Though the historic foundations of Taoism can be trace back to this ancient period, the three earliest written accounts of the Taoist ideology were composed during the Warring States Period. The authors of these works were: Lao Tzu, Kung Fu Tzu, (or as he is more commonly known, Confucius), and Chuang Tzu. Taoist philosophy truly affected the evolution of Buddhism once it found it way to China.

Lao Tzu

Lao Tzu, though the date of this legendary figure's birth is unknown, his death is recorded to have taken place in 604 BCE. The name Lao Tzu can be literally translated into, *"Old Boy."* This translation is, however, a bit too literal for its colloquial meaning to truly be understood. In English, the name, or more probably title, would be more precisely translated into, *"Old Knower."*

Legend states that Lao Tzu was the keeper of the Royal Archives at Loyang, in the capital of the Chinese Ch'u Empire. Few actual details of his life are known. He was a reclusive wise man, reluctant to found a school or gather a following. Lao Tzu became despondent over the continued wars that took place during his lifetime. He decided to leave the Ch'u capital and wander out into the wilderness, which would promise certain death. As he was leaving, he was persuaded by a gatekeeper to write down his thoughts for the good of mankind. This he did, which produced the most defining work of Taoism, *"The Tao Te Ching."*

The Tao Te Ching is made up of eighty-two single page chapters. This book details a profound way of viewing life, nature, and the universe. Its opening passage states, *"The Tao that can be told is not the eternal Tao. The name that can be named is not the eternal name."* With this simple, yet definitive statement the essence of Taoism is formulated. From this passage the practitioner understands the subtle nature of this philosophy and the paradox of life itself.

The Tao Te Ching describes a way of existing in non-action. It details that action removes one from the ultimate understanding of Tao and, thus, bars one from obtaining deepened enlightenment. This doctrine teaches that the more physical action one takes the more one is removed from the ultimate perfection of the universe. This is a philosophy that deeply permeates Zen Buddhism.

Confucius

Kung Fu Tzu, more commonly known as Confucius, was another personage who helped to lay the foundations for Taoism and Chinese culture on the whole. Kung Fu Tzu was a descendant of Shang Kings. He is believed to have been a younger contemporary of Lao Tzu.

Kung Fu Tzu's contribution was much less dramatic to the overall growth and definition of mystical Taoism than that of Lao Tsu's. Kung Fu Tsu's philosophy worshiped Heaven and was full of magical rites used to invoke and please the Chinese Gods. He wrote of the divine qualities of State loyalty and servitude to the Kings and their court. To the Chinese masses, Kung Fu Tsu's work is the most representative form of practiced Taoism. From feudal Chinese society onward, his writings have been used to define Chinese statesmanship and have directly influenced later generations of Korean and Japanese political regimes.

Chuang Tzu

Chuang Tzu was the third individual who's written work substantially defined Taoism. It is believed that Chuang Tzu was an official in the Lacquer Garden of Meng in Honan Province around the fourth century BCE. Chuang Tzu took the philosophic ideology of Taoism, prescribed by Lao Tzu, and further defined the doctrines of mystical Taoism using logic as a basis for thought.

Chuang Tsu's written work is generally referred to as, *"The Inner Chapters."* The Inner Chapters, while metaphorically detailing how a Taoists should encounter the world, is done so in a very literary fashion. Chuang Tzu writing is both religious and mystical. It details the way in which an individual should encounter every aspect of life in terms of making each action a sacred movement. To the individual who walks the spiritual path, this allows him or her to understand that each movement one takes leads them closer to an understanding of true-self and the divine. Thus, no physical action should ever be taken with out complete presence of mind.

Inspired by the teaching of Lao Tzu and Chuang Tzu there was a strong tradition for Taoist sages to retreat from the material world. The earliest Taoists often led solitary lives in remote reaches of China—often times living in mountain caves. Their lives were filled with meditation and living in harmony with nature.

Yin and Yang

The concept of Yin and Yang is no doubt one of the most integral theories in understanding the ancient Chinese mindset towards life and the universe. This fundamental concept of universal duality can be traced as far back as the Eighth Century BCE.

The Yin and Yang philosophy was developed by thinkers who watched all aspects of the functioning world that surrounded them. They came to the conclusion that all life exists within a duality. There can be no day without night. There can be no hot without cold. There can be no life without death. With this theory as a central focus, the Chinese philosophers expounded that everything is in a constant state of flux attempting to find a balance between these two polar dualities.

In Yin and Yang philosophy, Yin is the positive, where Yang is the negative. Yin is the earth. Yang is the heavens. Yin is cold. Yang is hot. Yin is female. Yang is male. Yin is emptiness. Yang is fullness. Yin is white. Yang is black.

Within the symbol that came to represent Yin and Yang, there exists a white dot in the black and a black dot in the white. This is to demonstrate that within all Yang is the essence of Yin. And, within all that is Yin, there is a trace of Yang. Throughout the continuous evolution of the world, these opposites give birth to one another.

In Taoism life is viewed in terms of harmony between the forces of Yin and Yang. Illness is an imbalance of the two. Yin and Yang are equal powers but are in constant motion, causing continual change. To remain healthy and in tune with nature in order to achieve a proper balance in the body thereby gaining the ability fully interact with the universe one must continually redefine the balance between Yin and Yang.

Though Zen Buddhism does not directly apply this understanding of duality, it does embrace this ancient mindset in continually seeking a balance is all that one undertakes. This is accomplished by finding a natural harmony in all of life's movements.

China and Buddhism

As Buddhist philosophy moved into China, it began to embrace various aspects of the Chinese schools of philosophic ideology, particularly Taoism. Therefore, the influence that Chinese philosophic thought played in the development of Zen Buddhism cannot be overlooked.

The Transmission of Enlightenment

The legendary Buddhist monk Bodhidharma, referred to as, *"Ta Mu,"* in Chinese or, *"Daruma,"* in Japanese, is the individual who laid the mystical foundations for *Ch'an Buddhism* or, *"Zen,"* as it is known in Japanese. The enlightened legacy of Bodhidharma can be traced directly to Siddhartha Guatama, the Sakyamuni Buddha. The path of enlightenment hailed by the Buddha was directly transmitted in an uninterrupted lineage through twenty-seven enlightened masters until it was handed to Bodhidharma in the forth century CE.

The lineage of enlightenment that was given birth to by Siddhartha Guatama is as follows:

1. Siddhartha Guatama
2. Mahakasyapa
3. Ananda
4. Sanavasa
5. Upagupta
6. Dhritaka

7. Micchaka
8. Buddhanandi
9. Buddhamitra
10. Bhikshu Parsva
11. Punyayasas
12. Asvaghosha
13. Bhikshu Kapimala
14. Nagarjuna
15. Kanadeva
16. Arya Rahulata
17. Samghanandi
18. Samghayasa
19. Kumarata
20. Jayata
21. Vasubandhu
22. Manura
23. Haklenayasas
24. Bhikshu Simba
25. Vasasita
26. Punyamitra
27. Prajnatara
28. Bodhidharma

The Life of Bodhidharma

Bodhidharma (440–528 CE) was born in Kanchipuram, India, near Madras at the beginning of the sixth century to a Brahman family of royal heritage. Bodhidharma became a student of the

Buddhist monk Prajnatara as a young boy and studied with him until he was thirty-eight years of age. Prajnatara was the headmaster of the Sarvastivada Sect of Buddhism. The Sarvastivada Sect was a school of Buddhist thought that practiced a more expansive approach to Buddhism than did the other traditional Indian Buddhist schools of the time. At the age of thirty-eight Bodhidharma was dispatched to China to relieve the missionary Indian Buddhist monk, Bodhiruci who was in charge of the Shongshan Buddhist Monastery—commonly referred to in the modern era as the Shaolin Temple or *"Shorin-ji"* in Japanese.

This temple was located in the foothills of the Shongshan Mountains. The Shongshan Monastery was the location where Indian monks would train Chinese monks in the teachings of the Buddha and would translate Sanskrit and Pali Buddhist texts into Chinese. Thus, this monastery was central to the disbursement of Buddhist knowledge throughout China and later throughout all of Asia.

As abbot of the monastery, Bodhidharma's teachings were simple and straightforward. He taught, *"Keep yourself away from relationships, as relationships bind one to the body and the mind."* And, *"Have no desires in your heart and you can merge with the Buddha."*

Buddhism and the Chinese Martial Arts

Upon arrival in China, Bodhidharma found that the monastic life had left the Chinese monks weak and in ill health. To remedy their physical condition, he taught them a series of exercises that legend states laid the foundation for the Chinese martial arts.

Formalized combat skills had obviously existed in China long before the arrival of Bodhidharma. These fighting techniques were, however, limited to those engaged in by the military. What historically occurred with the training of monks in fighting techniques was that the skills of the martial arts were no longer solely in the hands of professional warriors. From this initial introduction, numerous schools of martial arts developed in the Chinese Taoist and Buddhist temples. Each of these schools formalized their own techniques and possessed their own unique understanding of the martial arts.

The Birth of Zen

While in China, Bodhidharma is credited with laying the foundation for what was to become Ch'an Buddhism. *"Ch'an"* is the Chinese term that translates into the Japanese word, *"Zen."*

Though Bodhidharma is credited with laying the foundations for Zen, his teachings never really took hold and never truly flourished until much later in Chinese history. None-the-less, Bodhidharma detailed the fundamental teachings that eventually gave rise to Zen Buddhism. Though the philosophic understanding which came to be known as Ch'an Buddhism was not yet formalized, its inception is attributed to Bodhidharma. To this end, Bodhidharma is recognized as the First Chinese Patriarch of Ch'an.

Hui-ko

Near the end of Bodhidharma's life he passed his transmission of enlightenment onto Hui-ko (484-590), known as, *"Daiso Eka,"* in Japanese. Hui-ko became the Second Chinese Patriarch of Ch'an.

Hui-ko was a zealous student of Bodhidharma who continually asked his guru for guidance. For years Bodhidharma ignored all of Hui-ko's questions—teaching him that enlightenment was not something that could be given. Instead, an individual must come to embrace enlightenment through his own intensive meditative understanding.

It is recorded that on a stormy night, Hui-ko again came to Bodhidharma for guidance, asking, *"I have tried for years to quiet my mind master, but my mind can not find peace. I beg of you, can you please pacify it for me."* Bodhidharma answered, *"If you bring your mind to me, I will silence it for you."* After pondering Bodhidharma's statement, Hui-ko said, *"I can not find my mind, Master."* With this realization Hui-ko became enlightened.

Seng-ts'an

Seng-ts'an (d.606), known as, *"Konchi Sosan,"* in Japanese, came to Hui-ko when he was over forty years of age. He said, *"I have lived a long life full of sin Master. As I am now old, I cannot hope to reach enlightenment in this lifetime without your help. Please purify my sins."* Hui-ko answered, *"Bring you sins before me and they will be removed."* Seng-ts'an said, *"But Master, I can not find them." "Then you are free, my son."* Seng-ts'an immediately experienced instantaneous enlightenment and became the Third Chinese Patriarch of Ch'an.

As Ch'an Buddhist ideology began to become formalized in China, its understandings started to be presented in a more metaphysical manner than that of previous Buddhist writings. Seng-ts'an wrote a small book of his enlightened knowledge shortly before his death. It was titled, *"Hsin Hsin Ming," "Verses on the Faith Mind."* It opens with the passage: *"The path of enlightenment is easy for those who have no desire. When one does not love nor hate, then the truth instantly becomes clear and unclouded."*

Tao-hsui

Tao-hsui (580-651), *"Dai Doshin,"* in Japanese, was a young Buddhist monk when he came to pay homage to Seng-ts'an. When he received his audience with the Patriarch he commented, *"Please show me your compassion Master and guide me to the gate of divine liberation." "Who has bound you, my son,"* asked Seng Ts'an. *"No one has bound me." "Then you are already liberated,"* exclaimed Seng-ts'an. With this passage Tao-hsui experienced instantaneous enlightenment. He became the Forth Chinese Patriarch of Ch'an.

After Tao-hsui's enlightenment he lived for ten years in the Tai Lin Su Monastery. He then left the Temple and settled on Mount Shuan Feng, where he spent the next thirty years meditating and teaching his disciples the path to Buddhist enlightenment. Tao-hsui's meditative method was based upon, *"The Prajnaparamita Sutra."*

The Prajnaparamita Sutra

The Prajnaparamita Sutra is an essential Mahayana Buddhist text. This canon teaches that enlightenment comes through the complete emptying of the mind. It was created in India and was translated into Chinese by the Indian Buddhist monk Lokaraksa in 179 CE. Though this sutra had been translated for centuries, it was not widely accepted into Chinese Buddhist methodology. The methods presented within its text were, instead, practiced only by a limited number of reclusive Chinese Buddhist monks. This is predominately due to the fact that the Buddhist monks of this time period believed that enlightenment was a goal achieved through proper actions and proper meditation. As such, the concept of mental emptiness presented in the sutra was not readily understood.

The concept of emptiness detailed in the Prajnaparamita Sutra is similar to the Taoist mystical understanding of *"Wu," "Nothingness."* At the point when Tao-hsui began to teach the interrelationship between these two philosophic understandings is when the foundations for formalized Ch'an Buddhism were firmly set into motion in China.

Tao-hsui taught that enlightenment was already present in the individual, one simply had to realize it. In Japanese this understanding is known as, *"Sokushin Sokubutsu."*

Tao-hsui taught that enlightenment was not something that could be gained from studying the sutras or transmitted by a Buddhist master. Instead, enlightenment could only be realized by practicing severe austerities: by not speaking, reading the sutras, eating only the bare necessities, and meditating alone for a least thirty-five years with the mind focusing on divine emptiness.

Huang-jen

Huang-jen (601-674), is known as, *"Daimon Konin,"* in Japanese. He was the Fifth Chinese Patriarch of Ch'an. His pathway to enlightenment began when he was six years old and became a Buddhist monk in the monastery of Tao-hsui. Huang-jen, even as a child, was naturally inclined to spend his days in tireless meditation. As he matured, he was asked several times to come to the Imperial Court to become the counsel of royalty. In each case he turned down the invitation. He eventually located himself on the Ping-jung Mountain where he spent his days meditating and instructing his disciples.

Huang-jen composed the manuscript entitled, *"Tsui-shang-ch'un-lun."* In this document Huang-jen details that he did not believe in the sudden path to enlightenment. Instead, he taught that one should experience a gradual focusing of the mind through seated meditation. *"The Tsui-shang-ch'un-lun"* details that the zealot should meditate upon the place where the horizon meets the sky. The reason for this is that the Chinese number one is illustrated with a single horizontal line, which is similar to this visual illustration. This oneness of man, nature, and the Buddha is what the practitioner must seek. By focusing on this location, the meditator is given a reminder to his purpose for meditation.

Hui-neng

Hui-neng, known as, *"Daikan Eno,"* in Japanese, lived from 637 to 713 CE. His father died when he was a young boy and he supported his mother by cutting wood from a nearby forest and selling it in his town of Kuang-chou, modern day Guong-zhou. One day the young Hui-neng heard a man reciting a Buddhist doctrine. The passage was from, *"The Vajrachchedika,"* *"Diamond Sutra."* The monk sang, *"Let your mind go free, do not bind it to anyone or anything."* Hui-neng stated that upon hearing those words he was instantly enlightened. With further inquiry as to the source of the sutra the young Hui-neng was told it was recited by the over one thousand disciples of Huang-jen. With this, Hui-neng found a man to lend him some money for the support of his mother and he traveled to the Tung-shun Monastery of Huang-jen to seek deeper enlightenment. At this monastery Huang-neng meditated for many years.

Upon coming to understand that his own physical death would soon be at hand, Huang-jen, the fifth patriarch of Ch'an, asked his disciples to compose a poem, detailing their understanding of enlightenment. All the monks of the monastry believed that the senior disciple of Huang-jen, Shen-hsiu would no doubt win this spiritual poetry-writing contest and be awarded their masters seal of enlightenment.

Though Hui-neng could not even write, he employed the help of another monk and composed his poem. When Huang-jen heard all of the works, he knew that Shen-hsiu did not possess true enlightenment. Instead, he immediately understood that Hui-neng was the one who understood the true Buddha-mind.

Huang-jen did not reveal this to his disciples, however. Instead, he went to Hui-neng at night and awarded him his seal of enlightenment, which was symbolized by presenting him with his robe and his bowl. Huang-jen, knowing of the jealous nature of his disciples, told Huang-neng to travel south and wait for the appropriate time to reveal his enlightenment and teach the Dharma.

Legend states that Huang-neng traveled for two months with vengeful disciples in hot pursuit. When he was finally caught and accosted by the disciples lead by Hui-ming, a former general in the military, he simply threw the robe and the bowl on the ground, stating they were only physical objects and not the true symbol of enlightenment. With this, Hui-ming realized the true enlightenment of Huang-neng, fell to his knees, and asked him to become his teacher.

Hui-neng eventually ascended to the status of the sixth patriarch in the direct line of enlightenment transmission from Bodhidharma. His school became known as, *"The School of Sudden Awakening."*

Hui-neng emphasized that one must embrace the spiritual emptiness of their original Buddha-nature. He taught non-duality and the oneness of all elements of this universe. He insisted that one must make meditation are part of every element of the life and not simply allow it to a seated discipline. Many considered Huang-neng the actual founder of Ch'an (Zen) Buddhism, as it is through his teaches that the formalized techniques of Zen were set in motion.

Chapter 4
Buddhism in Korea

Formalized Chinese contact with the Korean Peninsula began in approximately 200 BCE, during the Chinese Qui Dynasty (221-206 BCE). This contact was intensified by the placement of Chinese military colonies on the Northern Korean Peninsula during the Han Dynasty (202-220 BCE). From these contacts the Korean Peninsula was led into a period of rapid advancement in agriculture, health science, military strategy, and formalized governmental statesmanship. In addition to Taoism; Confucianism, and later Buddhism were all introduced into Korea from China.

Due to the advancements on the Korean Peninsula, brought about by the introduction of the Confucian Doctrines and growing individual tribal unities, three Korean tribal kingdoms formed: Paekche, formed in 18 BCE, Koguryo in 37 BCE, and Silla in 57 BCE. This was the beginning of what became known as the *"Three Kingdom Period"* of Korean history.

Buddhism entered the Korean Peninsula state of Koguryo in 372 CE, at the hands of the Chinese monk, Sun-do. Sun-do was sent from the Chinese state of Ch'in on an official mission of Buddhism introduction. Though not quickly embraced by the Royal Court or the populous,

Buddhism did find a slow path to acceptance in Koguryo.

The East Indian monk Malananda introduced Buddhism to the Korean state of Paekche. Malananda arrived in Paekche, via China, in 384 CE. Upon his arrival he was met with an elaborate welcome from the Royal Court of Paekche.

The Paekche Royal Court had a very close relationship with its Chinese neighbors. From this contact, the Confucian doctrines and advancements in medicine had been introduced into this kingdom. Therefore, Malananda's arrival was heartily anticipated and his teachings quickly embraced.

To further the ongoing expansion of Buddhist thought, throughout the kingdom of Paekche, the Korean Buddhist monk Kyo-min returned from studies in India in 526 CE. He brought with him the Sanskrit Buddhist scriptures known as, *"Vinaya."* At the point of his return, he began translating this scripture into Chinese. This was the language of the Korean Royal Courts at this juncture of history. These translations helped to set the stage for the ongoing expansion of Buddhism on the Korean peninsula from this point forward.

By the time Buddhism was introduced into the Korean states, Chinese religious culture and society had already found acceptance several centuries before. From these early transmissions was born the formations of royal aristocratic Korean kingdoms. Thus, when Buddhism came to Korea, via the hands of Royal Chinese envoys, it was accepted into the Korean Royal Courts of Koguryo and Paekche with little adverse discourse. The Korean state of Silla was the exception to this process, however.

Silla did not readily accept the Buddhist doctrine. It held fast to the Confucian aristocratic ideology and to its native indigenous religion. In fact, attempts at the introduction of Buddhism were initially met with open hostility.

The Buddhist monk, A-do, in the beginning of the fifth century began to have success with the introduction of Buddhist ideology into the Kingdom of Silla. Rural peoples in the outlying regions of the kingdom were the first to accept the Buddhist idealogy.

In 527 CE King Pop-hung of Silla finally formally accepted the Buddhist doctrine into his county. This occurred when the King's closest minister, Ich-adon passed away. This action was preformed more as a tribute to Ich-adon, who was a practicing Buddhist, and as a method to quite the political rumblings of the common peoples, rather than as a means to formally prescribe to the philosophic ideals of Buddhism.

Though King Pop-hung attempted to secure the acceptance of Buddhism into his Kingdom, his efforts were met with great hostility from the hierarchical royal aristocracy of his court who

48

enjoyed the privileges of the Confucian school of thought. Buddhism was not fully accepted by the Royal Court of Silla until it had been practiced for a century by the other two Korean states of Koguryo and Paekche, and by the common inhabitant of the Silla Kingdom for several decades.

The Korean Buddhist Warriors

Due to the fact that Buddhism grew hand-in-hand with the warring cultures of the Korean Peninsula, it is impossible to diminish the influence that the seemingly two very different avocations had upon one another. None-the-less, due to the fact that Korean Buddhism was greatly ushered into Korean culture at the hands of warriors, this factor cannot be overlooked in understanding the birth and dissemination of Korean Buddhism.

During the Sixth Century the three Kingdoms on the Korean Peninsula continued to draw sharp cultural lines between themselves and the expansionistic Chinese T'ang Dynasty (618-907 CE). From this was born an extended period of war on the Korean Peninsula which gave birth to the Hwa Rang Warriors.

The Hwa Rang, *"Flowering Youth Warriors,"* were first presented to the Court of King Chin-hung in the Korean Peninsula Kingdom of Silla in 576 CE. King Chin-hung, whose given name was Sammaek-chong, was the nephew of

King Pop-hung who had first attempted to introduce Buddhism into Silla fifty years before.

The Hwa Rang were based in the Buddhist doctrine of no-self. They believed that their current human form was only a portal, whereby through proper Karmic action they could raise their consciousness onto their higher level of Buddha-self. Thus, these warriors did nothing for themselves. Instead, they devoted their entire lives, and all of their actions, to their supreme spiritual teacher, Won Hwa, *"Original Flower."* This teacher guided the Hwa Rang down the path of Buddhist warrior knowledge.

The original Hwa Rang were chosen in infancy on the peripheries of the kingdom of Silla. This was the highest honor that could be bestowed upon a child, as they were to spend their lives in what was believed to be direct service of their kingdom and the Buddha. Once chosen, the children were schooled in the doctrines of Ki, *"Internal Energy,"* healing, Buddhism, and martial warfare. By they time they reached their late adolescence, not only were they proficient healers and warriors but had spent long years engulfed in meditation.

At the point the first group of Hwa Rang were unveiled to King Chin-hung, and their expertise revealed, he became certain that these warriors were the means to defeat his attacking neighbors. Though years of war, King Chin-hung's soldiers were unable to defeat Silla's geographical neighbors: Koguryo, Paekche, and the invasive T'ang Chinese. Therefore, the Court of King Chin-hung set about to organize a group of young talented noblemen who could become Hwa Rang. The criteria for membership were those individuals who were exceedingly loyal to the thrown and were willing to be extensively trained in all forms of martial warfare.

The Royal Court of Silla, during the early reign of King Chin-hung, was still based predominately upon a Confucian doctrine of society. King Chin-hung realized, however, that the Buddhist Canon led to a more sterile mindset than that of Confucianism. In fact, in his later years, King Chin-hung actually became an ordained Buddhist monk, thereby symbolizing his true devotion to this religion. From this basis, King Chin-hung came to believe if he could band together a group of young noblemen who could be schooled in Buddhist ideology and all forms of known martial warfare, they would make the most superior combatants.

As wealth and aristocracy was prevalent throughout Silla's Royal Court, King Chin-hung found it difficult to find young willing participants to enter the strict order of the Hwa Rang. Thus, King Chin-hung initial method to lure young noblemen into the Hwa Rang was to enlist the help of two beautiful court women to gather men around them. The names of these two girls were

Nam-mo and Chun-jung. Several hundred young noblemen did, in fact, congregate in their presence.

Chun-jung became jealous of Nam-mo, however. She poisoned her wine and threw her into the river, killing her. The Silla Royal Court subsequently put Chun-jung to death and the group of men surrounding them disbanded.

The next method used to induct young noblemen into the Hwa Rang was to choose handsome males of royal birth. The age of these boys was as young as twelve years old. These men were then dressed in the finest clothing, and their faces were attractively painted with elaborate make-up. They were then extensively instructed in Buddhism, medical science, poetry, and song. It was believed those who fared well in these activities had the grace to become advanced warriors. Thus, a certain amount of them were recommended to the Court of the Hwa Rang.

The Hwa Rang were then trained in all known forms of martial warfare. They were taught the advanced practices of meditation, making each of their physical movements, a service to their leader and an action ultimately in service of the Buddha. It was the belief of the Hwa Rang, that meditation not only took place in the traditional fashion, in a sitting posture, but meditation was also achievable when one focused their personal spirit and then entered into battle with a highly refined purpose and vision of a victorious outcome. Thus, the battles the Hwa Rang fought became a spiritual exercise in enlightenment.

To the Hwa Rang, the necessary killing of an opponent was beneficial to the ultimate Karmic good of their society. From the necessary mortal actions they took, the Hwa Rang believed that they would gain good Karma and be raised to a higher incarnation in their next birth.

The Hwa Rang were the first organized group of monks to take the understanding of Ki, align it with Buddhist meditation, and perform what were considered supernatural feats. Legend states, that due to their developed ability to channel Ki energy at will throughout their body and their non-attachment for their physical form, they could propel their bodies into the fierce current of freezing Naklong River in the dead of winter and not be phased by the cold. Additionally, they could sit in deep meditation in the snows of the Taebaek Sanmaek Mountains, clothed only by a loincloth, and emerge unscathed.

In must be understood that during this period in Asian history, there were numerous societies of Buddhist monks who retreated from the world and choose to kill no form of living life either as a food source or as a means of self-defense. This is what set the Hwa Rang apart from other formalized groups of Buddhist monks. Their tradition taught them that the kingdom of Silla was the land of the *Maiterya, "The unborn Buddha,"* and as such, killing for their society was, in fact, a holy act. Therefore, the Hwa Rang believed that each life they took, in necessary combat, was a movement of meditation and would lead them onto Buddhahood.

Once a Hwa Rang was fully trained, he was put in command of a military troupe composed of several hundred common soldiers. From the battles won by the Hwa Rang, came the unification of Korea.

The unification of Korea occurred in approximately 660 CE. After this unification and the defeat of the invasive Chinese T'ang Dynasty, the mind of the Korean peoples rapidly began to shift from confrontations to more philosophic thoughts. The Hwa Rang, as a warrior group, fell into decline but not before Korean interaction with Japan provided a framework for the formation of what has come to be known as the Samurai. For a time, due to their refined knowledge of *Ki* and healing abilities, they became known as a group specializing in Buddhist philosophy, healing, music, and poetry.

Hyang-ga, *"Native song,"* was the gentle rhythmic poetic songs sung by the Hwa Rang. These songs, written by Hwa Rang or Buddhist monks, were believed to be vehicles for healing and creating divine intervention in human situation. The early Buddhism of Korea held tightly onto its reverence for divine intervention through the ever-present spirit world, thus, the music the Hwa Rang sung was done so for the purpose of worldly and Karmic healing. The Hwa Rang survived until the end of the Seventh Century when there is no longer any evidence of their existence.

The Silla Dynasty

At the point the Korean peninsula became a unified kingdom, Buddhism rapidly spread across the land. This period of Korean history is known as the Silla Dynasty. This dynasty existed between approximately 668 and 935 CE.

With the governmental acceptance of Buddhism, many Buddhist religious monuments, temples, and monasteries were constructed in the ensuing years after the unification of the Korean peninsula. The foundational essence of many of these temples remains in existence today.

The Five Schools of Korean Buddhism

With a universal acceptance of Buddhism, five primary schools of Buddhism came into existence soon after the formation of the Silla Dynasty. They were:

1. The Vinaya School
2. The Nirvana School
3. The Avatamasaka School
4. The Yogacara School
5. The Popsong School

Each of the founders of these schools, except one, would travel to China where they would immerse themselves in the teachings of a specific sect of Buddhist study. Upon return to their native Korea, they each established a school that set the evolution of Korean Buddhism and ultimately Zen Buddhism in motion.

The Vinaya School

The Korean Buddhist monk Cha-jang founded the Vinaya School of Buddhism. *"Vinaya,"* is a Sanskrit word that means, *"Discipline."* The mindset of expansive personal and mental discipline was used as the foundation to create this school of Korean Buddhism.

The Vinaya School is categorized as being part of the Theravada tradition of Buddhism. At the root of this school's teachings are the two hundred and twenty-seven rules of discipline, known in Sanskrit as, *"Pritimoksha."* These rules detail that the true Buddhist must overcome all forms of lust and worldly desire in order to reach the ultimate goal of enlightenment.

The Nirvana School

The Korean Buddhist monk Po-dok founded the Nirvana School of Buddhism during the early years of the Silla Dynasty. The teachings of this school were based upon one of the essential texts of Buddhism, *"The Mahaparinirvana Sutra."* This scripture is also known as, *"The Nirvana Sutra."*

In Chinese, this text is referred to as, *"Neipai Jing."* In Japanese, it is known as, *"Nehangyo."*

The Mahaparinirvana Sutra is a Mahayana Buddhist text. This text is believed to hold the final teachings of the Buddha. At the heart of this text is the Buddhist concept of emptiness and no-self. It teaches that one must let go of all forms of the known in order to merge with the Buddha-mind. Due to its contextual basis, this sutra has come to be one of the primary influences upon the evolution of Zen Buddhism.

The Avatamasaka School

The Korean Buddhist monk Ui-sang (625-702) founded the Avatamasaka School. Prior to his creation of this sect of Korean Buddhism, Ui-sang spent nine years meditating and studying Buddhist scriptures in China.

Ui-snag based his teachings upon, *"The Avatamasaka Scripure."* This scripture is known in English as, *"The Flower Ornament Sutra."*

The Avatamasaka Sutra is a large Buddhist scripture made up of numerous volumes based upon the Mahayana understanding of Buddhism. The Avatamasaka Sutra depicts the path of the Bodhisattva. The Bodhisattva is the Buddhist who is walking the road to enlightenment.

This scripture teaches a mystical perception of reality that was oftentimes expressed in the paradoxical. It focuses upon the concept of spiritual emptiness. It details how the mind of the practitioner unfolds as they approach cosmic consciousness.

The Yogacara School

The Korean Buddhist monk Chin-yo is the founder of the Yogacara School of Korean Buddhism. *"Yogacara,"* sometimes written, *"Yogacharya,"* literally translates from Sanskrit as, *"Practicer of yoga." "Yoga,"* in this case, refers to human union with cosmic consciousness. This sect is also historically known as, *"The Popsung School of Buddhism,"* in Korea.

The Yogacara School is a sect in the Mahayana tradition of Buddhism. *Yogacara Buddhism* bases is techniques upon the acceptance that all of this world is, what is known in Sanskrit, as, *"Maya,"* or *"Cosmic Illusion."* The Buddhist practitioner can only rise to the level of encountering Nirvana by denying this reality and all physical objects. Only then, will they see through the veil of Maya and emerge as an enlightened being.

The Popsong School

Won Hyo (617-686) created, *"The Popsong,"* or *"The Dharma Nature School of Buddhism."* Won Hyo is a legendary figure in Korean history. His school of Buddhism became the most influential school to begin in this chaotic period of Korean history and ultimately lay the foundations for Korean Buddhism up until the modern day.

It is believed that Won Hyo was born in the town of Zain-myon in the Kyongsang Province of Korea in 617 CE. During this period of time the struggle between the three Korean kingdoms was still under way and Won Hyo experienced the backlash from this period of war and restructuring. Though there are many legends talked about this historic figure, it is known that he was the one founding father of Korean Buddhism that did not travel to China to receive his training.

Legend states that Won Hyo became a Buddhist monk early in his life. He studied with numerous teachers but find none of them to hold the ultimate truth of enlightenment. He decided that he must travel to China to study with, what were considered, more advanced master of Buddhism. He left on this journey with his friend Ui-sang. While en route, they spent the night in a tomb. In this tomb, he experienced enlightenment. With this, he saw no need to continue his journey to China. Instead, he set about writing and teaching his unique understanding of Buddhism.

Whereas all of the other Buddhist schools, which came into existence during this period of Korean history, are directly associated with a specific Buddhist scripture, the Popsong School is not. It is understood that Won Hyo was a freethinker and innovator. Thus, he created a style of Buddhism that was directly adapted to his people.

Though it is known that Won Hyo was a prolific writer, only about twenty of his writing survived into the modern day. Many of the Won Hyo documents were destroyed during the brutal Japanese occupation of Korea between 1909 and 1945, where the Japanese occupying forces set about destroying all aspects of Korean culture.

The Koryo Dynasty

With the initial five schools of Korean Buddhism in place, Buddhism spread across the Korean countryside and was heartily embraced. This Buddhist expansion was aided by ongoing contact between Korea and China.

By the beginning of the tenth century of the Common Era, the Silla Dynasty began to come to an end. The sects of Korean Buddhism also begin to splinter and draw sharp lines between themselves. By this point in time, there were nine separate sects of Korean Buddhism that stood in sharp contrast to one another. This division was known as *"The Nine Mountain Sects."*

The Silla Dynasty was finally overpowered and the Koryo Dynasty (935-1392) was set in motion. One of the primary focuses of the Koryo Dynasty was to centralize and bring together the various sects of Buddhism that existed across the Korean peninsula. To help in achieving this, many members of the Royal Families and the

Aristocracy entered the religious order. The Korean Buddhist monk Uich-on (1055-1101) is an ideal example of this trend.

Uich-on was the fourth son of King Munjong (1046-1083) of the Koryo Dynasty. One of Uich-on's primary focuses was to bring the various schools of Korean Buddhism together. The problem Uochi-on experienced, however, was based in the fact that these various schools of Buddhist teaching had such diverse dogma attached to them that it was virtually impossible to make these schools accept a central teaching. Thus, though there was some restructuring, a unified Korean Buddhism did not emerge.

Chin-ul

In the twelfth century, it was the Korean Zen Buddhist monk Chin-ul (1158-1210) who would become instrumental in finally causing the various schools of Korean Buddhism to move towards a closer unity. In addition, from his teachings the Zen tradition of Buddhism came to be one of the primary schools of Buddhist thought on the Korean peninsula. From his successes, Chin-ul emerged as one of the most definitive proponents of Korean Buddhism.

Chin-ul: The Early Years

Chin-ul became a monk in training at the age of seven. At fifteen he was ordained a novice in a sect of Korean Zen Buddhism. By twenty-five he had passed all requirement to move forward in the Korean Buddhist monastic hierarchy. Yet, unhappy with the degenerative Korean Buddhist community, he walked away from his position.

Chin-ul decided to retreat to the mountains in hopes of finding the true essence of Buddhism and experiencing the ultimate knowledge of enlightenment. While in the mountain he had three distinct experiences of Nirvana. The first came when he completed reading, *"The Platform Sutra,"* composed by the Chinese patriarch Hui-neng. The second came upon the completion of reading the interpretation of, *"The Avatamasaka Sutra,"* by the Chinese Buddhist monk, Li Tong-xuan. The third and final experience of enlightenment came when Chin-ul complete reading, *"The Records of Dahui."*

At the age of thirty-two, with his enlightenment complete, Chin-ul emerged from the mountains and began to teach and bring together the various schools of Korean Buddhism. Though he too encountered obstacles, he settled at the Kojo Monastery and substantiated his school, known as, *"The Community of Concentration and Wisdom."*

As his students expanded, the Songwang Sa Monastery was constructed for him to expound his knowledge. At the monastery, Chin-ul, wrote, taught, and gathered many disciples.

The method Chin-ul used to unite the various schools of Korean Buddhism was based on his understanding that the essence of the Buddhist teachings were all the same—that each group is striving towards the ultimate experience of enlightenment. As such, though different schools may use varying techniques, these techniques should not set the followers of the Dharma apart.

Though division stills remained in the Korean Buddhist community, through the ongoing efforts of Chin-ul these schools became much less hostile towards one another. They ultimately embraced the understanding that though their paths to enlightenment may be different they all walked the path of the Dharma.

Though Chin-ul became highly respected among the masses, due to the fact that he never acknowledged a direct teacher-disciple relationship with any of the established masters, and, as such, the confirmation of enlightenment was never directly passed on to him, he was never truly accepted by the Royal Court of the Koryo Dynasty. None-the-less, Chin-ul followed the path of the Buddha, experienced his own enlightenment, and formalized the teachings of Buddhism in Korea. From his teachings, the understandings of Zen and Zen enlightenment have continued to be handed down for centuries on the Korean peninsula.

Chapter 5

The Evolution of Zen Buddhism in Japan

Buddhism traveled from Korea to Japan in 536 of the Common Era. This introduction took place in association with a political delegation sent by the Royal Court of Paekche in order to substantiate ties with the island nation. Among the gifts that were presented to the emperor was a statue of the Buddha and a group of Buddhist scriptures. The Japanese Royal Court did not readily appreciate these gifts. None-the-less, in the nature of statesmanship, a shrine was constructed for their storage.

After Buddhism was initially introduced into Japan from Korea, the further transmission of Buddhist knowledge came predominately from China. Over the next half century Buddhism came to be embraced by the Japanese Royal Court.

Whereas, in China and Korea, the general populous embraced Buddhism before it found its way into governmental acceptance, this was not the case with Japan. In Japan, from its early foundations forward, Buddhism was systematically disseminated to the people by the government. For the most part, the population of Japan held closely to their native Shinto religion that was predicated upon ancestor worship, gods, goddesses, spells, and amulets, and only marginally accepted Buddhism.

The Heian Period

During the Heian Period (794-1185) Buddhism began to take hold in Japan. The governmental capital of the nation was located in Kyoto at this juncture in history. From here, two distinct school of Buddhism came into existence and began to flourish across the nation. They were the Tendai and Shigon Schools of Buddhism.

The foundational basis for the Tendai School of Buddhism can be traced to Tao-hsuan (702-760). Tao-hsuan was a Chinese Buddhist monk who arrived in Japan at the age of thirty-five and became the teacher of the Japanese Buddhist monk Gyohyo (722-797). Gyohyo became the first teacher of Dengyo Daishi (767-822). Dengyo Daishi is also known by the name, *"Saicho."*

Dengyo Daishi

Dengyo Daishi left Japan and traveled to China in 804 in order to gain advanced knowledge of Buddhism. In China he studied at the temple on Mount Tiantai. This temple was the location of the highly revered T'ien T'ai sect of Mahayana Buddhism. After remaining at the temple for he a year, Dengyo Daishi was returning to his native Japan when he met a Chinese priest, Shun-hsiao.

Shun-hsiao taught a methodology that employed many esoteric and metaphysical rituals in this brand of Buddhism. He initiated Dengyo Daishi and gave him possession of a thirty-eight-volume canon of teachings. Dengyo Daishi returned to Japan and began to teach this new, and unique style of Buddhism.

In Japanese these Buddhist rituals came to be called, *"Mikkyo."* And Dengyo Daishi's teachings became most commonly referred to as, *"The Taimitsu School of Buddhism."* This sect is sometimes referred to, however, as, *"The Mikkyo School,"* or *"T'ien T'ai,"* or, *"Tendai Buddhism."*

Dengyo Daishi's dissemination of these techniques helped to draw the Japanese populous into the practice of Buddhism. This occurred due to the fact that these elaborate rituals closely paralleled those employed by the native Japanese shamanistic religions. With a foundational basis for acceptance now in place, Buddhism became more readily accepted by the masses.

With a common point of acceptance as an impetus, Buddhism followed a slow and labored path of ongoing growth and acceptance throughout Japan. It was not until the twelfth century, after the Gempei War, however, when the Royal families were displaced and military rule came over Japan that Buddhism would come to be truly embraced.

With its ongoing acceptance and integration in Japanese culture and society Buddhism has continued on its path of expansion throughout the centuries in on this island nation. With this, Ch'an Buddhism came to be introduced into Japan from

China. Upon its arrival, Ch'an Buddhism, which, as detailed, is known as, *"Zen,"* in Japanese, found a very fertile soil for its ongoing growth and evolution.

The Schools of Zen

There are two primary schools of Zen Buddhism that have evolved through the centuries and are practice in Japan today. They are the Rinazi and the Soto Schools of Zen Buddhism. Myoan Eisai founded the Rinzai School and Dogen Zenji formed the Soto School.

Eisai

Myoan Eisai (20 April 1141 – 5 July 1215) is known primarily as Eisai Zenji in Japan. Eisai formed the Rinzai-shu or Rinzai School of Buddhism. In Chinese this sect is known as Linji Zong or Lin-chi Tsung.

Eisai Zenji was born in the Bitchu province of Japan. Like many of his contemporaries, Eisai was schooled in Buddhist ideology from the time of his birth forward. Eisai possessed a unique and overwhelming calling to these teaching, however, and from an early age he began to define his life by these understandings.

Eisai began his formal studies of Buddhism at the Tendai Temple in Japan. He quickly became dissatisfied with the state of Buddhist thought in Japan at this juncture of history, however. This was in no small part to the ongoing rivalries and infighting among the various temples and sects. In 1168 Eisai traveled to Mount Tiantai in Southeastern China for a period of approximately six months. As previously detailed, Mount Tiantai was the home base for the T'ien T'ai sect of Mahayana Buddhism in China.

Zhi-yi

The Tiantai sect is known as, *"The Lotus Sutra School."* The text, *"The Lotus Sutra," "Suddhamanppurna,"* in Sanskrit or *"Myo'ho Renge Kyo"* in Japanese, is one of the essential Mahayana Buddhist scriptures. This text was written approximately two hundred years after the death of the Buddha and details essential elements of the Buddhist pathway to enlightenment.

The Chinese Buddhist sage Chen Zhi-yi (538-597) founded the T'ien T'ai school of Budhism. He is credited with being the first to systematically classify the Buddhist canons. His motivation for doing this was to find the source element of the teaching of the Buddha. This was due to the fact that by the sixth century the teachings of the Buddha had already split into so many varying understandings that there was no single common teaching. Thus, Zhi-yi set about on the path to find the essence of the Buddha in all of the writings that had been laid down before him. From his organizational advancement he is understood to be the first Chinese teacher to truly break away from the foundational Indian teachings of Buddhism and to formalize a uniquely set of Chinese perimeters.

While at Mount Tiantai, Eisai first encountered the teaching of Ch'an Buddhism. After a brief return to Japan, Eisai again traveled to China—eventually mastering the techniques of Ch'an Buddhism and receiving his certification as an enlightened teacher. In 1191 he returned to Japan and founded the first Zen temple in Japan, the Hoonji Temple in Kyushu, Japan.

The Japanese Royal Court did not embrace the new style of Buddhism Eisai was teaching, however. Due to this fact, Eisai spent many years attempting to gain recognition from both the Royal Court and the traditional Japanese Buddhist scholars. Eisai did not find widespread acceptance of Zen Buddhism until in 1199 he left Kyoto for Kamakura where his teachings became heartily embraced by the Shogun and the warrior class samurai.

The Rinzai School Today

Throughout the centuries, the Rinzai School of Zen has continued to evolve. Today, it is the smaller of the two primary sects of Zen Buddhism, in Japan. It is divided into fifteen primary schools defined by the fifteen temples, which embrace this style of Zen.

Dogen

Dogen Zenji (19 January 1200 – 22 September 1253) is the founder of the Soto School of Zen Buddhism. Dogen was born in a mountain village near Kyoto, Japan. His father, Koga Michichika, was a Minister to Minamoto no Yoritomo. This is the man who brought about the first Samurai Shogunate—military rule over Japan. Dogen's mother was the daughter of a Regent from the Fujiwara Royal family. Thus, Dogen was born into a family of very high standing.

Dogen's father died when he was two and his mother passed away when he was seven. Dogen had been drawn to spiritual writings all of his life and at the age of twelve he secretly left the home of his paternal uncle, with whom he was living, and traveled to Mount Hiei where his maternal uncle, Ryoken was a monk at the Shuryogon-in Temple. After a year of apprenticeship Dogen took his formal vows of renunciation at the Enryaku-ji Temple and was given the name Buppobo Dogen. He later formally changed this name to Kigen Dogen.

Dogen initially absorbed himself in the study of the Tendai School of Buddhism. Due to the excessive expansionistic militaristic mentality and corruption of his temple, however, Dogen was unfulfilled. His teacher Koin suggested he go to China and study Ch'an Buddhism. In 1217 Dogen traveled to Southern China to study Ch'an under Eisai's successor, Myozen (1184-1225).

In addition to Myozen, Dogen studied Ch'an from two very prominent Ch'an masters of the Ta-hui sect, Wu-chi Liao-pai and Chi-weng. During his period of apprenticeship Dogen came to realize that the Ta-hui school was too closely linked to the governing hierarchy of China and it was affecting its practitioners. Thus, he became disillusioned and left their temples. Finally, Dogen met Ch'an master Ju-ching of the Tsao-tung sect. Ju-ching provided Dogen with a true pathway to enlightenment. After five years Dogen returned to Japan with Ju-ching's Seal of Enlightenment. As he was a prolific writer his message spread throughout Japan and Zen Buddhism came to be embraced by the masses.

Dogen taught a method of Zen that propagated a return to the old method of Zen, expounded upon in, *"The Tenants of Pai-chung."* This doctrine was the oldest existing Chinese text written on the fundamentals of Ch'an practice. In addition, he taught that one should, *"Just Sit,"* in meditation, contemplating the emptiness.

Dogen believed that there was one path to enlightenment and that was Zazen, *"Seated meditation."* He taught that meditation was the way all of the previous illuminated beings had achieved enlightenment. Therefore, seated meditation was absolutely necessary for one to reach Nirvana.

In a text composed by Dogen, *"Shobo Genzo Zanmai o Zanmai,"* he stated that there are three types of meditation. They are: *"Shin no Kekkafu Za,"* the sitting of the body, *"Shin no Kekkafu,"* the sitting of the mind, and *"Shinji Datsuraku no Kekkafu Za,"* the sitting of the body and the mind as one unit. Dogen believed that the ladder was the only pathway that promised Nirvana.

PART II

The Philosophic Foundations
of Buddhism

The principals of Zen Buddhism are founded upon a specific set of doctrines, laid down by the Buddha. These doctrines guide the practitioner towards a deeper understanding of self, the universe, and the universal-self, also known as the Buddha-mind. These teachings are not structured in religious dogma. Instead, they are a set of guidelines that the Zen Buddhist can adapt to their own specific set of life circumstance and use as a means to move towards a more consciousness interaction with life and ultimately reach the goal of enlightenment.

Chapter 6
The Four Nobel Truths

At the core of the Buddhist tradition is, *"The Four Nobel Truths." These* teaching were originally recorded in the Pali Canon. Though other historic texts from the same period mention nothing about this discourse, the Pali Canon claims that these words are the first teaching of the enlightened Siddhartha Guatama.

Whether or not this will ever be historically substantiated is unimportant. What is important is that the Buddha is credited as having provided these teachings that have been practiced for centuries.

The Four Nobel Truths set the stage for what have become the essential teachings of the Buddha. To this end, they can be viewed as the root of Zen.

The Four Nobel Truths are:
   1. All beings are bound by Karma.
   2. The cause of suffering is desire.
   3. Obtaining enlightenment can alleviate suffering.
   4. Enlightenment is obtainable by practicing the Eightfold Path of the Dharma.

1. All beings are bound by Karma.

The Sanskrit word, *"Karma,"* literally translated, means *"Action."* This word represents the law of cause and effect, *"As you sew, so shall you reap."*

Karma

Karma is one of the most complicated and profoundly philosophical issues each person must deal with in understanding Zen Buddhism and, in fact, life. This is because of the fact, right and wrong, good or bad, are not universally defined in this physical world. Not only does each culture possesses a somewhat differing view of right and wrong but each person holds their own values and individual perceptions of good and bad. Certainly, there are distinct wrongs: hurting someone unnecessarily, forcefully taking something from another person, behaving selfishly, and so on. But beyond these obvious instances, the precise definition becomes lost. For example, what about when you hurt someone unintentionally? Or, while pursuing the spiritual path you must leave someone behind, thus, causing him or her to suffer at your absence?

The question of Karma is amplified when people justify the wrongs they are performing for what they believe to be a just cause. For example, how many people have died in wars on this Earth motivated by religious idealism?

Perhaps even more disconcerting is the case of individuals who continually cause physical and emotional pain to other people. Yet, somehow their life seems to continue forward in an unhindered path of success and acquisition. When justifying their negative Karmic actions these people oftentimes allude to the fact that they had a bad childhood, are getting back at the world for what was done to them, or due to negative peer influence they were guided down the wrong road. Though these may be psychologically valid rationalizations, none-the-less, negative actions have taken place, often times injuring good people.

On the other side of the issue, there are those individuals who continually provide a positive service to the world. Yet, they are confounded by continued negative encounters. Why should adverse experiences happen to these people if they are expounding good to humanity?

The philosophic debate on the nuances of Karma has gone on for centuries. And, it will continue. In ancient Vedic scriptures, three levels of Karma are defined which may provide some insight into the various types of Karmic actions. The three levels of Karma are:

1. *Sanchita Karma, "Accumulated Karma."*
2. Prarabdha Karma, *"Actions which create Karma."*
3. Kriyamana Karma, *"Current actions."*

Sanchita Karma

Sanchita or *"Accumulated Karma"* is the Karma that you have previously substantiated. *Sanchita Karma,* not only defines actions that you have taken in this life, but also actions that you performed in previous incarnations. Many believe that this is one of the primary components that go into the formation of an individual's personality—as they are acting out a lifestyle and mindset that they substantiated in a previous life.

The understanding of *Sanchita Karma* is also used to define why seemingly good people encounter negative events in their life. It is understood that though they may now be very good, in a previous existence they must have created adverse Karma. Thus, they suffer in this lifetime.

Certainly, in the Western world, the concept of paying for sins from a previous life strikes an adverse chord in many people. This is because of the fact that they believe that their current body is their only body and even if they do accept the theory of reincarnation, why should they have to pay the price for an existence that they no longer have any control over? This is where the belief systems indoctrinated by religion comes into play in the definition of Karma. For example, a Buddhist would simply let go of philosophic questioning and relinquish him or herself to accepting the understanding of *Sanchita Karma* as fact. Thus, any life occurrence, be it positive or negative, is quickly rationalized and accepted as Karma.

Prarabdha Karma

Prarabdha Karma is the Karma that has come into existence due to past actions. Illustrative of this type of Karma is the individual who performs negative acts, for what ever physical, emotional, or psychological rational, and then later in their life they encounter unfavorable situations. These events may take place in the next life, the distant future, or may happen almost instantaneously. This understanding provides some solace to people who have been wronged by others, as they know, sooner or later, that unjust individuals will have to pay the price for their actions.

It is additionally understood, at this level of Karmic understanding, if one's Karmic debt is paid up, then any Karmic retribution for a negative act will be incurred relatively quickly, as there is not a long backlog of wrongs waiting to be repaid.

Prarabdha Karma not only details the events that occur as a result of adverse Karma, but it is also equally applicable to positive Karma, as well. This can explain why the rare case of a truly negative person, in this life, continually encounters seemingly positive experiences; they were a very good person in a past life.

Kriyamana Karma

Kriyamana Karma is the actions you take that lay the foundations for either positive or negative Karma in the future.

Some people were born into economically poor living conditions, dysfunctional families, or have had a childhood corrupted by bad influences and occurrences. Others have experienced a relatively positive childhood only to be impacted by negative situations, as they have grown older. For decades, Sociologists and Psychologists have attempted to draw conclusions to why an individual follows a particular path in life based in their foundational attributes. Though there is, no doubt, quantitative validity to some of their findings, it must be ultimately understood that we each are the masters of our own destiny. At any point in life, be it before you instigate any adverse Karma or post having unleashed a plethora of negativity, you can take back your life and choose to consciously move forward—doing good things for the world, creating good Karma, even while you suffer the inevitable repercussions for actions you have taken in the past.

Certainly, most of us have encountered influences in our lives that were not of the purest content. Additionally, due to innumerable psychological factors we have all walked down impure paths with people we should not have. Under these influences most of us have all performed acts that we now can see as, *"Bad*

Karma." Knowing this, you have two options in your life. One, you can hold on to those experiences and allow them to set a pattern for the rest of your life. Two, you can consciously let go of the past and move forward into a world where you will never allow negative people or situations to guide you again. With this more positive approach, you allow yourself to live each new moment of life in a positive fashion; following the path to self-realization while you do good things for all those you encounter.

Creators of Karma

From ancient Vedic scriptures we learn that once one's personality is initially set in motion by Sanchita Karma, the individual then moves forward into life choosing to act out one of three types of Karma: Sattva, Rajas, or Tamasa. These three types of Karma parallel the understanding, known in Sanskrit as Gunas, or *"The Three States of Consciousness."*

Sattva is the pure state. Rajas, is the active, passionate state. Tamas is the dark, overripe state.

The Sanskrit word, *"Karman."* is used to describe an individual who is creating a specific type of Karma. Thus, an individual is a Sattva Karman, Rajas Karman, or a Tamas Karman.

The Sattva Karman's actions are pure, precise, and directed towards a higher good, each step of their life. A Rajas Karman's actions are all performed from a sense of ego—everything is done for the betterment of him or herself. A Tamas Karman's actions are performed from a dark, deluded, and confused state of mind—serving no one and no thing.

Karma and the Human Being

Existing in a human body means that everyone, no matter how holy, is bound by Karma. It must be ultimately understood that no act is wholly good and bad. What may benefit one may cause pain to another. Thus, as we are bound by the complexities of human existence and good and bad will remain an individual's perception.

The Zen Buddhist does all that he or she can do to create a positive world: forgiving those who have hurt him or her, helping those who need help, guiding those who need guidance. Any action is attempted from only the purest of motivations. Understanding that, ultimately, each person is their own person, with their own emotions, desires— cultural and psychological influences.

You cannot make everyone happy. Thus, the Zen Buddhist walks their path, embracing life and attempting to do the most possible good each step of the way.

2. The Cause of Suffering is Desire.

The second precept of the Four Nobel Truths is, *"The Cause of Suffering is Desire."* This statement is so elementally true that in its simplicity, little more need be said.

Desire is your choice. You can choose to live a life believing that you do not possess enough material wealth, power, physical beauty, love, or enlightenment. If you choose to believe that your life is lacking, then you will cause yourself to be constantly in pursuit of these desires. This will equal a life devoid of peace.

Your second option is that you can settle into the Zen understanding of, *"Divine Perfection."* This is the simple acceptance of cosmic perfection that is readily available to all of us.

By accepting the Divine Perfection you allow yourself to understand that you are enough, have enough, and are exactly where you should be in the grand scheme of reality. By consciously accepting the Divine Perfection of this universe you allow yourself to exist in a state of peace, which gives birth to the pathway to Nirvana.

3. Obtaining enlightenment can alleviate suffering.

Central to the core of Buddha's teachings is the understanding that we, as human beings, are all walking towards the ultimate goal of enlightenment. This is true whether or not we are moving towards it consciously or unconsciously.

It is important to keep in mind that enlightenment, referred to in Sanskrit as, *"Maha Bodhi,"* meaning, *"Great Awakening,"* did not originate with the Buddha. This understanding was in existence since the dawn of advancing human consciousness.

The Pali Canons of Buddhism record that there were twenty-eight Buddhas, or enlightened beings, which existed before Siddhartha Guatama. The numbers of those, who have obtained this ultimate level of human consciousness, have continued to multiply throughout the centuries.

Walking the conscious path towards enlightenment is a personal choice. You must make this decision very consciously and pursue it diligently, never allowing your mind to lose focus upon your objective—objective not desire.

The path to enlightenment begins from an untold number of motivating factors. Once on this path, a spiritual teacher, several teachers, or a philosophic belief you hold deeply in your heart may guide you. As you progress along the mystical road of Zen, you will come to realize that all of the formalities you initially held onto, your religion, your teacher, and even your own images of self begin to fall away. What remains is a pure being that is no longer bound by the traditional desires and rationales of the material world. With this, *"Falling away,"* a pure new self emerges that embraces the essence of the Zen Buddhist philosophy, *"We all are already enlightened. We simply must remember this fact."*

With this, the objective of enlightenment is lost and the experience of enlightenment is found.

4. **Enlightenment is obtainable by practicing the Eightfold Path of the Dharma.**

The Eightfold Path is the prescribed method for each human being to forgo the constraints and limitation of material human existence and move closer towards interaction with Cosmic Consciousness. The Eightfold Path provides you with a method to transcend the limitations of the ego based mind and body and move to a realm where you are no longer defined by the temporary nature of this desire-based existence.

The Eightfold Path of the Dharma is:
   1. Right Views
   2. Right Intentions
   3. Right Speech
   4. Right Conduct
   5. Right Livelihood
   6. Right Effort
   7. Right Mindfulness
   8. Right Concentration

1. Right Views

Knowing what is right is not difficult. People choose to walk a path devoid of righteousness, based predominately upon their desires: desires for power, desire for control over others, and lust for acquisitions.

The first step in obtaining Right Views is to let go of your desires. With this formal mental action you become free from the programming that has previously infiltrated and controlled your thinking mind.

Embracing Right Views is not difficult. Let go of what society has told you is right. Let go of what your friends try to make you believe is right. Let go of thinking that what you already know is right and true rightness is immediately revealed.

2. Right Intentions

Why do you desire something? Why do you hope for its acquisition? Why do you hope for anything to be different than it already is?

The abstract promises of this material world can give you a million reasons why things in your life should be different. The person who follows the path Zen, however, accepts the ultimate perfection of this universe and desires to change nothing. Thus, their intentions are not focused solely upon self. Not focused upon self, individual intentions are not dominated by desire. Without desire they become free from Karma. Free of Karma, intentions become a pure expression of Zen.

3. Right Speech

People like to talk. People like to tell other people what they think, how they feel, and what they believe. People want to tell you their ideologies so passionately that you stop believing what you believe and start believing what they believe.

Words are based in ego.

How many times have you said something that you wished you had not said? How many times have you made a statement, and it came out wrong or was misinterpreted? The basis of this occurrence is words being spoken that are not actualized from a wholly pure space of consciousness.

There is an elemental problem with language. Each person possesses their own individual understandings and, thus, assesses their own interpretation to each statement that they hear. Therefore, what you mean to say may never be truly understood by another individual—as they are at a different level of evolutionary consciousness than yourself. It is for this reason that many spiritual ascetics stop speaking altogether. This state of spiritual practice is known in Sanskrit as, *"Mauni."*

Though this style of rigorous spiritual practice is not required, it is essential to keep in mind that if you are going to say something, make sure that the essence of your words comes from a space of purity. If you are understood, great! If not, do not attempt to argue your point, as the person you are speaking with does not possess the mind to hear what you have to say.

Remember, with nothing said, nothing is left unsaid.

4. Right Conduct

People may provide all kinds of definitions and excuses for the actions they take. The difference between Right Conduct and Wrong Conduct is that Right Conduct needs no explanation. What you have done, you have done; all who witness it understand its necessity.

How can you come to a space of knowing what is Right Conduct? If you have to think about your actions, they are not pure.

Through conscious cosmic interaction, gained by walking the path of Zen, you enter into a natural space of Right Conduct. What you do is what you do. What you do, needs to be done.

In this space of pure Zen consciousness, you will not need to think. Not thinking, your actions are obvious in their necessity.

5. Right Livelihood

There are more excuses made for the way an individual obtains their livelihood than any other physical action on this earth. The most common one is, *"I need the money."* But, why? If you did not permeate your physical existence with desires then your need for money would substantially decrease.

The problem with earning a living by means of an unconscious avocation is that what you are doing may be creating negative Karma and hurting the world.

How many people work at jobs that truly does damage to not only their own bodies but to other people and the world around us? Though the may not like their job, they continue forward because they have created a situation where they must have a certain income to meet their needs. Though this may sound like the natural course of events in a person's life, it is not, necessarily, the path of consciousness.

The leading problem that guides a person to not making a living from a conscious perspective is that they define their life by desires. Then, they become dominated by the ongoing necessity of paying for these desires. The result is a world fueled by people who are willing to do whatever it takes to get more money to pay for previously actualized desires and to obtain new, ever growing wants and needs.

The remedy, STOP! Take control of your life. Pay off your bills. Put your desires behind you and set about on the path of living consciously.

No doubt, you have already proven to yourself that any of your dollar based desired led you away from true happiness. Thus, you have no excuses to remain trapped by a world motivated by materialism. Let go.

Once you have entered into a more refined path of dollar consciousness, a means of obtaining a positive material existence will come to you. Then, you will be able to not only nourish your body and your soul, but the world around you, as well. You will be able to do this without ever creating any negative karma.

6. Right Effort

Effort is action. Action equals Karma. From every action there is an equal and opposite reaction.

Right Effort witnesses you performing actions that do not set the natural balance of your body, your mind, the earth, or the universe out of alignment.

How do you know if your effort is right? By witnessing the reactions. For example, if you meditate does it cause any person or object in your life pain? No, it does not.

If you become a vegetarian does any animal have to die to feed your hunger? No, they do not.

If you decide to walk, ride a bike, or roller skate to your destination, does your movement cause enhanced amounts of pollution to be unleashed upon this planet? No, it does not.

Your effort is your choice. It is more than simply deciding that you will sit in meditation at the same time each day. That is discipline. Your effort is how you choose to consciously interact with all forms of living and non-living beings. It is how you choose to embrace this world. It is how you choose to physically and spiritually exist at all levels.

Choose your Right Effort. Don't make excuses for yourself and you will know the right choices to make.

7. Right Mindfulness

It is essential to understand that at every level Zen Buddhism present life teachings in the form of a paradox. Zen presents its understandings in this manner because every aspect of Zen reveals to the practitioner a new level of understanding that uncovers the false self, ultimately revealing the true self that gives way to enlightenment. This concept is hard for many people to understand. This is why it must be understood that to understand Zen, you must accept the fact that everything you think you know is bound by the constrains of what is referred to in Zen as, *"Mind Stuff."*

Mind Stuff allows you to believe that you are embracing Zen simply because you study under a teacher, are attending a meditation class, or have been initiated by a Guru. Though these physical actions may ultimately guide you to higher mind, they are not the No-Mind that Zen embraces. They are simply things.

In Zen, thinking you are spiritual means that you are not spiritual. Thinking that you are good mean that you are not good. Believing that you walk the spiritual path means that you are not truly walking the spiritual path. This is the place where many novice practitioners become lost on their spiritual journey. They believe that by doing some physical action, of which meditation is one, they are becoming more refined and more holy. They are not.

Right Mindfulness is a very subtle issue on the path of Zen. If you believe you are being spiritual and are on the road to enlightenment, you are not.

How then can you achieve Right Mindfulness? By letting go of all the external physical images and especially all of the Mind Stuff that goes hand-in-hand with the spiritual path. With this, you will touch the essence of Zen and you will ultimate embrace the Zen understanding of No Mind.

No Mind is the spiritual state of existence where what you are, how you see yourself, who you desire to become are all relinquished. All that remains is the pure reflection of true self, referred to in Zen as the Buddha-mind.

How do you obtain this level of existence? Follow the path of no path—embrace the way of no way. This is Zen.

8. Right Concentration

The thinking mind is an interesting tool. How many times have you been in love and kept thinking about the person you are love with? How many times have you been lost in the realms of anger and you could not get your thoughts away from the person who angered you? How many times have you remembered a song, and it played over and over and over again in your head?

The thinking mind is a very formable resource. What you put into it and what you think about defines who you become. If you think about love, you find love. If you think about lust, you will be led down the road to encounter lust. If you think about the Buddha, the essence of the Buddha will become your state of mind.

Why? Because what you focus upon is what you will manifest in your life. What you think about is what you will find.

Similar energy attracts similar energy. If your mind is angry, angry people find you. If your thoughts are lost in the realms of lust, you will go to places where lust is prevalent, and you will encounter those of like mind. If, on the other hand, you think about the Buddha, people with a Buddha-mind are attracted to you.

Right Concentration is not easy. This is especially true due to the fact that those who inhabit this material world teach us to develop minds that race all over the place and think about a million things at once. This is why many spiritual teachers recommend a, *"Mantra," "Spiritual phrase,"* to their students. This gives them a single point of focus—a sound that they can turn to and constantly remind them of the spiritual mindset they hope to embrace.

Though you may be assigned a mantra or a mental image to focus upon, it is you who must make this a part of your life. It is you who must forgo negative thinking at all levels. No one, not your guru, not even the Buddha himself, can do this for you. It is something you must decided to do

This is why, at the outset, Zen is about you. It is about you refining who you think you are. Then, Zen transcends this level of self-consciousness and becomes about you loosing any limited perceptions of individuality and self that you may hold—ultimately leading you, (who is no longer you), to merging with the cosmic whole.

You must take the step. You must focus your mind. Then you must let go of you. This is Zen.

Chapter 7
The Five Precepts

In association with The Four Nobel Truths and The Eight-Fold Path, the practicing Buddhist embraces a set of disciplines that are known as The Five Precepts.

The Five Precepts are:
1. I will refrain for harming all living creature.
2. I will refrain from taking that which is not mine.
3. I will refrain from sexual misconduct.
4. I will refrain from incorrect speech.
5. I will not partake of intoxicants.

The Five Precepts are not a forced set of doctrine that a Buddhist must embrace. Instead, they are designed as a defined set of criteria that an individual decides to live by. By making the decision to consciously abide by these precepts, not only do you become a more spiritually refined person but come into closer contact with the universal Buddha-mind.

As one views The Five Precepts it can be easily understood that these are rules which any person can apply to their life—whether they are a

Buddhist or not. By embracing these ideologies an individual becomes not only more physically and mentally healthy, but they additionally become more emotionally and psychologically well balanced, as well. This is due to the fact that these precepts are not based in religious morals. Instead, they are designed as tools that can truly guide a person to a more whole and spiritually fulfilled life.

1. I will refrain for harming all living creature.

The first precept guides an individual away form the practice of harming other living creatures. Certainly, in our modern world, overpowering, overtaking, defeating, and becoming more than another person is a commonly sought after goal. *"Being more,"* is taught in virtually every self-help book and at every self-help seminar. People are told that living life in a state of simplicity is never enough. Instead, one must be bigger, stronger, more respected, and more powerful if they hope to truly be all that they can be.

But, where are these desires created? Are they formed from the pure state of the Buddha-mind or are they the creation of the programming unleashed by a modern society that exists on a plane of complete lack of peace? The answer is obvious.

With the understanding that those who focus their lives upon the material world are elementally different that those who focus their lives on the world of spirituality as the defining factor, each individual must determine how he or she is going to interact with other lives they encounter. Is this interaction going to be from a space of confrontation and acquisition? Or, is it going to be from a space of purity and compassion? This is a personal choice, and this is why the first precept causes a person to decide how they are going to interact with humanity.

Understanding the First Precept

If a person has not defined how he or she is going to encounter other living creatures, how can they ever look deeply into themselves and come to understand the subtler workings of the meditative mind? For this reason, the first precept causes a person to define whether or not they are going to cause this world to be a better place, by never meeting force with force, or are they going to base their life upon the desire to continually be more than others.

If a person is continually focused upon being more than others, then this person, by their own definition is going to live a life dominated by loss and gain. As long as the individual is achieving, then they will be happy and satisfied. But, when another person overpowers them and achieves their own goals instead, then this person's life will be set into chaos.

If you can embrace the most basic understanding taught by the Buddha, *"The cause of suffering is desire"* then you no longer will be dominate by the need to achieve the meaningless goals of life. With this as a basis, then the first precept becomes easily embraced because you will not need to hurt anybody or anything as you will be at peace with yourself and you will be moving through your life consciously interacting with all forms of life that you encounter.

Vegetarianism

Many Buddhist practitioners view this first precept as the defining factor for vegetarianism. Certainly, this precept may be interpreted in this manner. For the killing of life simply as a means of sensory gratification is not on pare with Buddhist ideology at any level.

The entire question of vegetarianism must be viewed from a deeper perspective, however, *"Are you basing what you eat on desire or necessary physical sustenance?"* This is a question that each person must answer for him or herself.

There is no right or wrong answer to the question. It is something that you must define fro yourself. Certainly, we can look to the life of the Dalai Lama and other Tibetan Buddhists who eat meat as part of their diet to understand that vegetarianism is not a strict Buddhist dogma.

Moreover, through the advances of modern science it is now understood that each piece of fruit and each vegetable is actually a living, thriving entity that possess energy. Therefore, does the eating of fruits and vegetables harm a living entity any less harm than the eating of animals?

Ultimately, what you eat is an element of your spiritual practice that you must define for yourself. A good question to ask is, *"Can you stay healthy and thrive with out the eating of meat."* If so, then that may be your clue to becoming a vegetarian.

2. I will refrain from taking that which is not mine.

The second precept addresses the simple understanding that one should not steal from other people. As universally accepted as this understanding is, stealing from other human beings is one of the most common actions which takes place in the human race—in all of the many forms that it takes. In fact, stealing is so common it has become idealized in many arenas of life. Some simple examples of this can be seen in the person who is given too much change by the store clerk and keeps it. Another example is the business owner who thrives by charging more than is necessary for his products. A person who plagiarizes the research or creative work of another is also wrongfully taking something that is not theirs. Or, the individual who physically or mentally overpowers another person and then takes pride in their actions is also taking something that does not rightfully belong to them.

Taking what is not rightfully yours sets the negative wheel of Karma in motion. No matter how justified or ego-filled you may feel from your actions, what is right in this world is right and what is wrong is wrong.

Ultimately, taking what is not yours it based in one primary factor, desire. People desire money, so they are willing to do whatever it takes to get it. People desire easy accomplishment, so they are willing to steal the works of others to make themselves appear more accomplished. People desire power, so they are willing to do whatever it takes to gain physical and mental control over other people; by whatever means necessary.

With desire as the central focus, what is accomplished by stealing is never based in the teachings of Zen. Instead, all that may be accomplished, by wrongfully taking from others, is formulated by the ways of the non-spiritual world.

With desire as the motivating factor, all that can be set in motion is a pattern of negative karma. And, negative karma never leads to Nirvana. For these reasons, the Zen Buddhism consciously walks through life, analyzing each of their action, refusing to be controlled by the demands of society and peer pressure. From this, they are allowed to make their own decision, based in mindset of consciousness. With a mind focused on the good of all humanity, personal desires fall away, eventually giving birth to the Buddha-mind.

3. I will refrain from sexual misconduct.

Sexuality is one of the most complicated issues in regard to walking the spiritual path. This has especially become the case in this modern era when many of the restraints of sexuality have been lifted and sex is no longer viewed as an evil activity, as it was in times past. In fact, for the most part, sexuality has become heartily embraced.

It must be understood, however, that the person walking the path of Zen Buddhism does not formulate their thought patterns based on the ways of the world. Instead, they are focused on achieving a more spiritually fulfilled life, ultimately leading to Nirvana. For this reason, sexuality must come to be viewed from a new, more enlightened perspective for it to be completely understood.

First of all, sex is not bad. Sex is what has given birth to mankind, and it is a completely natural action. Aberrant sex, however, is not good. The definitions of aberrant sex are obvious. And, there is no need to detail or discuss those areas.

The reason the subject of sex must be consciously addressed, by the practicing Zen Buddhist, is the fact that sex is based in desire. With desire as the central focus, the action of sex losses its root essence and moves to the realms of worldly desire. This is the factor that has guided many Buddhist, throughout history, to leave behind the material world and relocate themselves with the walls of monastery.

Protected by a temple and supported by the spiritual brotherhood and sisterhood that goes hand-in-hand with dwelling in such a location, the Buddhist may forget the bodily needs so heartily embraced by society and focus their life upon meditation. Though this is the path chosen by some, it is by no means a prerequisite to all those walking the path of Zen Buddhism.

For most people, the path of Zen Buddhism allows them a method to step away from the controlling hands of the world and learn a new method to deal with and view this place we call life. By taking this conscious action an entirely new world of possibilities opens up and a person may view this world from a much purer and more understanding space of consciousness. For this reason, the rudimentary biological function of sex must be addressed and personally defined in the mind of each individual who is walking the path of Zen Buddhism.

With desire as the basis of sex, the Zen Buddhist realize that given the opportunity this desire possesses the potential to control a person. For this reason, the individual walking this path chooses the opposite and consciously makes the statement, *"Sex will not control me."* With this statement formalized in the mind, how then does the Buddhist move away from the controlling hands of this elemental desire? It is a simple change of focus.

As one walks down the path of Zen Buddhism, they quickly come to realize that their thought patterns have been formed by the influences they have encountered throughout their life. As a Buddhist, they learn that they must take control of these thoughts if they hope to interact with Nirvana.

It is that simple. Take control of your thought. When you find yourself thinking a though based in desire, STOP IT! Think about something else. Or, simply sit down, focus your mind, and enter into a meditative mindset.

It is you who decides what you think. You can think about anything that you want. No one can tell you what to think. It is you who possess total control. Choose to use this control and you will decide what you want to think about. With this control activated in your thinking mind, not only do you gain control over your physical life and your physical desires, but you come to understand that with a focused mind you can easily leave behind any unwanted desires, including the desire for sex.

4. I will refrain from incorrect speech.

Certainly, we can all agree that talking has led to many of the problems of this world. People voice their opinions. Everyone has a right to hold an opinion. But, your opinion may not be mine and mine may not be yours.

Ultimately, it is easy to understand that opinions are based on an individual's perception of this world. And, what one person believes to be fact may not coincide with another person's understanding. This goes from large-scale religious and political ideologies to the most mundane areas of life.

Talking causes disagreements. And, disagreements are the cause of all kinds of chaos in this place we call life.

What the Zen Buddhist comes to realize is that any perceptions they may hold are simply based in beliefs. Belief is not based in truth—it is simply based upon a particular individual's understanding of a particular situation. But, this does not make it true, it only is what somebody believes. Thus, it is only Mind Stuff.

Mind Stuff is not the root of Nirvana. As such, the Zen Buddhist does not allow him or herself to be dominated by it. Instead, Mind Stuff is understood to be what it is, simply a particular person perception of the world based on what that person has learned, studied, or been taught.

Mind Stuff is not born of the Buddha-mind. As it is not part of the Buddha-mind, the Zen Buddhist defines what they believe and then simply allows their beliefs to exist in the place in their mind that holds beliefs.

Beliefs are never allowed to control the mind of the Zen Buddhist, nor are they allowed to lead them to arguments or disagreements. They are simply defined and then seen for what they are, Mind Stuff. Thus, the Zen Buddhist never allows him or herself to be control by what they believe because they understand that with each new realization about life, beliefs will change.

As the age old saying goes, *"Silence is golden."* The Zen Buddhist prefers to be quite rather than to enter into conversation that may escalate into disagreements, which may end in war.

Be silent. This is Zen

5. I will not partake of intoxicants.

The fifth precept is one of the most easily understood doctrines on the Buddhist path. Intoxicants lead to an artificially alter state of consciousness. And, no matter how good this altered state may feel, it is not a natural occurrence and thereby does not lead to Nirvana.

Throughout history there have been prophets who claim that intoxicant lead to a higher state of consciousness. In India, the use of hashish is highly prominent. Many holy men can be seen smoking it. And, some of their disciples come to believe that the altered states which is encountered from its use is, in fact, a glimpse into the realms of Nirvana.

The American Indian mystics have long been known for their use of peyote, claiming that it provides mystical insight. And, the chemically manufactured drugs of the twentieth century, most prominently LSD, have been detailed as a means to obtaining enlightenment.

There are three things that any thinking individual quickly understands when coming to view the statements made about artificial intoxicants.

1. Artificial intoxicants are artificial. Even if they come from a naturally occurring substance in nature that does not mean that the visions they provide are organic.

If you must take something to achieve Nirvana, it is not Nirvana.

2. By taking an artificial substance you allow yourself to be controlled by that substance. There is no way to measure the effect a drug will have upon you.

Zen Buddhism is based on an inner knowledge arising from a deep awareness of the self. It is not based on putting something in your body that you have no control over.

Lack of control is the way of the world. Lack of control is not the path of Zen. Zen Buddhism is based on controlling the sublet elements of your mind, which ultimately leads to embracing the all-knowing Buddha-mind.

3. Artificial intoxicants do not last. The temporary nature of these drugs defines their lack of truth.

Nirvana is a state of being which embracing an all-knowing understanding of the universe. Once experience, it does not diminish, nor does it gradually fade away, like the wearing off of an intoxicant. Thus, the artificial alteration of the brain, no matter how good it may make you feel, is not the path of Zen

The Three Jewels of Buddhism

From the time of the Buddha forward, each individual who has walked upon the spiritual path has encountered their own unique set of obstacles that has caused them to lose their peace and be swayed from the Buddha-mind. It is the human condition of life; we each like what we like and dislike what we dislike. Until an all-encompassing understanding of reality emerges from encountering Nirvana, when we encounter something that we dislike, we become unhappy and are removed from a peaceful state of consciousness. To overcome these obstacles the practicing Zen Buddhist finds refuge in what are known as The Three Jewels.

The Three Jewels are:
> **1.** The Buddha
> **2.** The Dharma
> **3.** The Sanga

The Three Jewels are the three essential factors of the Buddhist path that cause the individual to refocus their consciousness and be guided down the pathway to Nirvana.

The Buddha

The Buddha is the source point of Buddhism. He is recognized as the ideal human being that has transcended the limitation of the lower self and has raised his consciousness to the supreme level of enlightenment. As such, the practicing Buddhist looks to his example as a means of understanding that all obstacles of this physical world may be overcome and that an individual may raise him or herself to interact with supreme consciousness.

As the centuries have progress the idealized image of the Buddha has grown and he has become, in many ways, more of a deity than simply that of an idealized example of an individual depicting the road to Nirvana. This was never the teaching of The Buddha, however. He never asked to be worship.

From this worship-orientated mindset, temples dedicated to and statues of the Buddha have spring up across the globe. Within these temples, you will find people that are worshiping and praying to the Buddha. Sadly, these people have truly misinterpreted the teachings of this great being.

The essence of the teachings of the Buddha is that people are whole and complete onto themselves—each person possesses the ability to elevate him or herself to embrace cosmic consciousness. By worshiping, a deity a person removes him or herself from self-awareness, however. By worshiping a deity, they become focused upon, *"Disciple consciousness."* This is perhaps the leading reason that more people do not find their own enlightenment, because the choose to worship instead of, *"Becoming."*

Therefore, when it is stated that one should take refuge in the Buddha, this does not mean that one should turn to him in times of need and pray. What it does mean is that one should follow the example of the Buddha, by looking deeply into self, finding the answers to one's shortcoming, refine them, and emerging an enlightened being.

The Dharma

Translated from Sanskrit, *"Dharma"* means, *"The way."* In Buddhism, Dharma refers to the spiritual path that the Buddhist is traveling.

When one takes refuge in the Dharma, what they are doing is being guided by the teachings of the Buddha. Therefore, when one experiences a state of strife, they look to The Four Nobel Truth, The Eightfold Path, and The Five Precepts for guidance.

Walking the spiritual path is not always easy. Simply because of the fact that one is walking the spiritual path does not mean that they are not bound by the realities of life that every other human being must also encounter. The Zen Buddhist must interact with the people, find a method to pay the bills and must have a place to sleep. With the life interaction it takes to achieve

110

these goals comes strife. This is life and it cannot be completely overcome.

What the Dharma provides the practicing Zen Buddhist, however, is a more effective way of dealing with the realities of the world. Instead of being overcome by the strife of the world, the Zen Buddhist is trained to look beyond the illusion of the material world and to focus their consciousness on the Buddha-mind. With this as a source point and the teaching of the Buddha providing a guide, the Zen Buddhist can maneuver their way through all of lives obstacles form a much more conscious and understanding perspective. Thus, the will pass through all of the obstacles of life without becoming overcome by them.

The Sanga

"Sanga," translated from Sanskrit, means, *"Association."* The Sanga is the spiritual brother or sisterhood of practicing Buddhist.

The Sanga is an ideal place to turn when one encounters problems, but it is also the source point for the evolving spirituality of the individual. From the Sanga one gains insight into life and Zen Buddhist consciousness as they are interacting with others who are walking upon the same path. In many cases, within the Sanga one will encounter those who have walked the path for a much longer period of time and, thus, possess advanced knowledge. Additionally, the Sanga provides necessary encouragement to overcome the obstacles that each person who follows the path of the Buddha will encounter.

Within Buddhism there are many teachings tools that have been laid down and refined for centuries. There is also a highly structured community that one can turn to for ongoing growth with the precepts of Zen Buddhism. With these support networks in place, each soul who walks the path of Zen Buddhism is helped in letting go of the constraints of modern society in order that they may ultimately embrace the Buddha-mind.

PART III
Zen Buddhism: The Meditative Practices

At the heart of Zen Buddhism is the practice of meditation. Meditation is a formalized technique where the mind is calmed, and the practitioner is allowed to come into contact with the Buddha-mind. It is understood that only through a perfectly centered mind is an individual ever able to merge individual self with the universal self and reach the ultimate state of human existence, enlightenment.

Zen Buddhism is not full of a plethora of meditative techniques as is the case with some of the other Schools of Buddhism. Though there are a few variations to the primary Zen Buddhist meditative practice of Zazen, they are all based in a single focal point—focusing the mind to the degree where it may encounter Nirvana.

114

Chapter 9

Zazen

Zazen is the practice of formal meditation. In Japanese, *"Za"* means to be seated. *"Zazen,"* therefore, means, *"To be seated in Zen."*

The practice of Meditation has been handed down for centuries as a method for one to come into contact with divine understanding. Zazen is the Zen Buddhist application of this ancient practice.

The Seat

In Zen Buddhism, meditation is referred to as, *"Shikantaza."* Literally translated, this Japanese word means, *"Just Sitting."* With this as a basis, in English, *"Zazen,"* is commonly referred to as, *"Sitting."*

It is understood that your seat, meaning the way you are sited, is one of the most essential elements in proper meditation. For this reason, the Zen Buddhism practitioner very consciously sits down and steadies themselves in their seated posture before they ever begin to meditate.

The Sanskrit word, *"Asana,"* is often used to describe the seated posture for meditation. Translated from the Sanskrit, *"Asana,"* means, *"Seat"* or *"Throne."*

The classic posture for seated meditation is, *"Padma Asana,"* or, *"The Lotus Pose."* This is where the practitioner sits cross-legged on the ground.

There are three variations of this posture. The first and most basic is, *"Sukh Asana."* This is where the legs are naturally crossed and the feet touch the ground underneath the thighs. The second is, *"Arddha Padma Asana,"* or *"Half Lotus."* In Japanese, this posture is referred to as, *"Hankafuza."* Hankafuza is where the top of one foot is brought up and placed on the thigh of the opposite leg.

The third meditative posture is, *"Padma Asana,"* or, *"Full Lotus."* In Japanese this posture is known as, *"Kekkafuza."* Kekkafuza is where the right foot is placed on the left thigh and the left foot is placed upon the right thigh.

For centuries it has been taught that Kekkafuza is the most beneficial posture to assume while meditating. It is stated throughout ancient texts that this pose is the most foundationally firm as it locks the body tightly into place and, thereby, allows the mind to focus solely upon meditation.

Though Kekkafuza is understood to be the ideal posture for meditation, it is uncomfortable for many individuals to sit in this position for extend periods of time. Ultimately, Zazen is about the practice of meditation. So, if you cannot comfortably sit in this pose for long periods of time, then you should sit in whatever position you can comfortably maintain, including sitting in a firm chair, as you perform Zazen.

Many times, the Zen Buddhist practitioner, when they are seated in any of the meditative lotus postures, will sit upon a small mat, known in Japanese as, *"Zabuton."* Upon the mat sits a small pillow, *"Zafu."* The practitioner then sits upon these two objects as they meditate.

Some schools of Buddhism believe that this creates too soft of a seat for a practitioner to truly meditate. Others believe that by adding a bit of comfort it will actually aid in the meditative process. Ultimately, it is you who must decide what works best for your body and your mind as you practice Zazen.

Seiza

The Zen Buddhist also uses another position for seated meditation, the kneeling pose. This posture is known in Japanese as, *"Seiza."* The kneeling posture is achieved by placing both of your knees on the floor, separated at the distance of your shoulders. The tops of your feet are encountering the ground, and your right big toe is placed atop the left big toe. Your spine should be kept erect, as with the lotus posture. Once you are seated in this position, you place your hands face down, naturally atop each of your legs.

Firm Seat

To correctly perform Zazen your body must be kept in a firm positioning. Your spine must be kept erect so your internal energy will continue to flow in a constantly ascending pattern.

The Japanese Buddhist term, *"Fudo no Shisei,"* means, *"Immovable Posture."* This is essential to Zazen. So, whatever meditative posture you decide to take, you must be able to firmly formalize your body into that posture and remain unmovable throughout your meditation. With a firm seat your mind can concentrate upon your meditation and not be distracted by physical movement or discomfort.

The Hands in Zazen

Once you have settled into your seated postures, it is important that you consciously straighten your spine. From this, your back muscles do not become strained, and energy is allowed to flow unimpeded up and down your spine.

With you body in a firm posture, you will then place your hands in what is known in Japanese as, *"Hokkaijo in,"* This means, *"Hands in perfect balance with the universe."*

The Japanese word, *"In"* is a translation of the Sanskrit word, *"Mudra,"* which means, *"To seal."* To form an In, you place your hands in a very precise formation.

The ideal Hokkaijo In for Zazen occurs when you lay your right hand in your lap with your palm open and facing upward. You place your left hand loosely on top of it. You then allow the tips of your thumb to lightly touch.

Hara

The Hara is the body's natural center of gravity. This bodily location exists approximately four inches below the navel. In addition, Hara is the bodily location where Ki, *"Universal Energy,"* congregates and is dispersed. For this reason, Hara is one of the most sacred locations on the human form.

Hara is located approximately four inches below the navel. From this central location it expands approximately two inches in each direction. In Buddhist scriptures Hara is referred to as, *"Tanden."* Tanden means, *"The burning place of energy."*

The Zen Buddhist practitioner of meditation understands that it is essential to become highly focused upon this revered location in order to not only readily tap into and utilize Ki energy but to additionally remain consciously balanced in all of life's activities, particularly meditation. For this reason, as one prepares for Zazen they focus upon this location and consciously find a balance in their seat before they begin the practice of meditation.

Open Your Eyes

Most people understand the various techniques of meditation to be performed with eyes closed. For obvious reasons, with your eyes closed you are less prone to be distracted by external images. Zazen, however, is performed with your eyes slightly open—loosely gazing at a visually stagnant location approximately three feet in front of you upon the floor. Some schools of Zazen place an actual dot on the floor in front of the practitioner in order to give them a physical placement of focus.

The reason the eyes are left partially open in Zazen is threefold. First of all, by leaving your eyes partially open you keep yourself associated with the fact that you possess a physical body. In Zen you never negate this fact, as do various schools of Yoga. Instead, you embrace the fact that your soul is located in a physical being and that this body is your pathway to the Buddha-mind. Secondarily, by holding your eyes slightly open you do not allow yourself to enter into a dream-like state of sleep, where your mind can drift to fantasies. Finally, it is understood that the process of Zen meditation leads one down the path to an acutely focused mind. By locking your vision onto a single spot on the floor, you train your thinking mind to become acutely controlled. From this, you possess much more authority over the experiences of your physical body and emotional mentality then does the average person.

You can, in fact, as the depth of your meditation increases, control such things as your physical and mental reaction to injury, pain, and emotionally debilitating life situations.

Wall Staring

In certain schools of Zen Buddhism, the technique of, *"Tai Ch'ng Pi Kwan"* or *"Wall Staring"* is used to achieve the objective of leaving your eyes partially opened while limiting the amount of possible external visual stimuli. In this case, the practitioner locates a spot on the wall slightly below eye level and locks their vision onto it and uses it as his point of focus.

Beginning Zazen

To begin Zazen, sit upon the floor and allow yourself to become integrated with your seated posture for a few moments. Once you feel stationary, firm, and comfortable, begin to observe your breath. Do not attempt to control it, simply allow it enter and exit your body, via your nose, naturally. Once your mind has grown accustomed to this process begin to attach the number One to each in-breath and the number Two to each out-breath. Mentally repeat, *"One," "Two," "One," "Two."*

It is understood that your mind will tend to wander when you first begin to practice Zazen. Mentally counting will help to bring back your concentration to the life-giving process of breathing.

Stop Thinking

The purpose of Zazen is to still your mind. Therefore, you do not want to think, visualize, or fantasize when you are practicing Zazen.

When you first begin the practice, thoughts will naturally form in your mind. For most of your entire life you have allowed your thoughts to rapidly move form one thought onto the next. Thus, your mind is trained to interact with life in this fashion.

If you find yourself thinking during Zazen, do not be upset with yourself, simply refocus your consciousness on your One, Two counting and again embrace the thoughtless Buddha-mind.

How Long?

Most schools of Zen have their students perform Zazen in a group session for forty-five to fifty minutes. This is understood to be the ideal amount as it provides the practitioner with enough time to truly focus their mind.

For the student who is in the early stages of Zazen practice, however, sitting for this amount of time is not required. This is especially the case, if the new practitioner is performing this technique alone.

The physical state of being alone and solitary is good for Zazen. This is due to the fact that alone, there is less chance of distractions. While sitting alone, however, it is understood that the mind of the novice meditator will tend to race from thought to thought more readily than if they are in a group. From this, the student may become disillusioned with their inability to meditate.

For this reason, when practicing Zazen alone in the early stages, it can be practiced for approximately twenty minutes twice a day—generally in the morning and in the evening. By performing Zazen for this amount of time, one can learn how to calm the mind and embrace the conscious emptiness of Zen without feeling forced to sit for an uncomfortable amount of time.

Hishiryo

The practice of Zazen allows the mind to become silent. Thinking is defined in Japanese as, *"Shiryo."* Not thinking is *"Fushiro."* Zazen, however, leads the practitioner to the more advance state of consciousness known as, *"Hishiryo," "Without thinking."*

Hishiryo is thought without thought. From this state, pure consciousness is encountered. When the individual embraces pure consciousness, the mind is not held captive by desire. Without desire the individual mind realize its own Buddha nature. From this, oneness with all elements of the universe is embraced.

When the mind is allowed to be silent, perfect action is accomplished. This is because of the fact that no action is attempted. Action within no action is the paradoxical essence of Zen.

The action of no action is the basis of enlightenment. Thus, Zazen is paramount to the development of the individual in Zen Buddhism.

Chapter 10
The Zen Koan

The Rinzai School of Zen Buddhism, founded by Myoan Eisai, teaches that enlightenment may come is a burst of instantaneous cosmic understanding. This school of thought details that though one must meditate to realize this ultimate state of human existence, the actual experience comes in a flash of consciousness. For this reason, the Rinzai School emphasis the use of the Zen Koan as one of the Primary pathways to enlightenment.

The Zen Koan is a statement generally presented in the form of a question. The Koan is designed to cause the Zen practitioner to alter their course of normal thinking and be forced into a new reality where the enlightened mind may be encounter.

A common example of a Zen Koan is, *"What is the sound of one hand clapping?"*

The early foundations of the Koan can be traced back to the Chinese Tang Dynasty (618-907 CE). In Chinese, the term Koan is, *"Gong-an."* This term originally detailed an established principal or accepted law. As the term evolved and became embraced by Zen Buddhist philosophy, this *"Established principal,"* came to represent the deeper understanding of cosmic reality.

The Practice

A teacher, known as *"Roshi"* in Japanese, presents a Koan to the student in a private session known in Japanese as, *"Dokusan."* The student then presents an answer to their teacher.

There is no one correct answer for a Koan. The answer given simply reflects the student's understanding of life, Zen, and enlightenment. The purest answers are understood to arise from the enlightened inner being of the student. For this reason, the answer is never thought-out. It is simply expressed.

In many cases, if the Roshi is not satisfied with the answer, he or she will instruct the student to go back and meditate on the Koan. This meditation is not the student taking the Koan back with them, sitting down, and trying to figure out the best answer. Instead, it is a process where the student meditates upon the Koan, until the essence of the Koan is embraced by the meditative non-thinking mind. At this stage, when the Roshi poses the Koan again, a new, purer answer is revealed. Ultimately, it is understood that the Zen practitioner will embrace Satori by peering deeply into the meaning of the Koan.

Chapter 11

Kinhin: Walking Meditation

Meditation is not limited to Sitting in Zen Buddhism. It is understood that the practitioner must ultimately bring meditation into every element of their life. For this reason, there are techniques of movement meditation that may be brought into the overall Zen meditative practice even in the early stages of a student's meditative development.

The Japanese term, *"Kinhin,"* describes a walking style of meditation. Kinkin is often times used in the Zendo, *"Meditation Hall,"* to give the meditative practitioner a break during long periods of seated meditation.

Kinhin begins when a bell in the Zendo rings twice. This occurrence is known in Japanese as, *"Kinhinsho."* At this point the Zazen practitioner arises and Kinhin begins.

The Practice

Kinhin is a very formal practice of walking meditation and is not simply a chance to stand up and loosen the legs. When the bell rings, the Zen practitioner arises very consciously while placing their left hand, in the style of a fist, into their right hand, which grasps this fist. This mudra is known as, *"Shashu,"* in Japanese. The eyes are lowed to the ground, just in front of the practitioner. The walking then very consciously commences in a clockwise direction around the Zendo. The steps are very small, and each one is taken with focused consciousness.

As with Zazen, the focus of Kinhin is placed upon the breath. In Kinhin a breath is taken in association with each step. The in-breath is very consciously taken in, and a small step is made. The out-breath is exhaled, as another small step is taken.

Moving Outward

Kinhin is not limited to simply walking around the Zendo. The conscious practitioner can elevate this meditative practice and bring it into each walk they take.

As Zen is a pathway of consciousness, walking in Kinhin can truly bring spiritually into new areas of your life. In fact, there are many modern schools of Buddhism that use Kinhin as one of their primary practices outside of the Zendo.

To make Kinhin part of your ongoing life meditation, all you have to do is remain very conscious of your breath as you move outside and begin to take a walk. Just as in Zazen, this takes some practice.

Practice is necessary, due to the fact when you are inside, in a quite environment, with no movement to distract you; it is much easier to remain consciously focused and to catch yourself when your thoughts begin to wonder. When you are exposed to the sights and sounds of the external world, it is much harder to remain consciously focused, however. This does not mean that you should not do it. In fact, by bringing your meditation out to the world, not only do you cause yourself to redefine your understand of meditation but you become a positive conduit to the material world around you.

Focusing

To take Kinhin to the outside world, you will ideally perform Zazen for at least a few minutes and very consciously focus your consciousness. You will want to mentally define what you are about to do. Once you feel you are appropriately centered, you will then very consciously rise, just as you would in the Zendo, and move towards the door.

Whereas in the Zendo you will clasp your left fist in your right hand, as you perform Kinhin, this is not necessary when you take your Kinhin out to the world. In fact, it is better that you do not bring undo attention to yourself, as this has the potential to invite distracts to your walking meditation.

While practicing Kinhin in the Zendo, you walk one small step per breath. When you take your Kinhin out to the world, this practice may be employed, but it is not required. This depends on your particular situation and the environment you find yourself in. If you find yourself in a very tranquil environment, then all of the formalities of Zendo Kinhin can be employed. But, if you are simply walking the streets of the city, the formalities can be left behind. All that need remain is your acutely focused meditative consciousness.

Beginning the Walk

To begin your walk, you will walk at the pace you find appropriate to your situation. You will begin by finding naturalness in your step. Your pattern of walking should not be forced. Simply allow it to be natural.

As you walk your heart rate will naturally increase, which will increase the intensity of your breathing. So, before you begin to become focused upon your breath, allow your body to find a harmony.

At the point you feel natural in your pace and in-tune to the beating of your heart, you will then start to consciously observe your breath. Do not force it. Do not control it. As this will cause your natural breathing patters to be altered and it could result in you becoming lightheaded from lack of oxygen or hyperventilated. Simply allow yourself to breathe appropriately to the pace of your walk.

At the point you have achieved a balance of body, mind, spirit, and breath, began to consciously observe your breath. As you walk, watch your breath enter your body, fill your being with life giving oxygen, and then exit your body. Never attempt to control it, simply focus your consciousness upon the process.

If you wish to add the countering of, *"One,"* *"Two,"* to your movement—as a means to remain meditatively focused, do so. With each in-breath, count, *"One."* With each out-breath, count, *"Two."*

As you walk, allow yourself to experience your environment, but do not allow yourself to be controlled by it. Accept that we live in the world and there are many things going on. You are a part of the supreme essence of this universe. Thus, you never have to be controlled by this illusionary place we call life.

Just as in Zazen, if you feel your thoughts slipping, bring them back to the focus of your breath. If you have to stop at a crosswalk for a passing car, simply witness the movement of life, but remain focused upon your breath.

By bringing meditation into new and uncharted elements of your life, not only do you learn to take positive control over your racing mind, but you also come into a deeper harmony with your universal-self. From this, you learn to maintain mental control in all life experiences—be they bad or good. You learn to remain meditative in all life situations and never be controlled by every changingness of this place we call life.

Chapter 12

Zen Buddhism and the Arts

Whereas many world schools of meditation focus their practices solely upon the individual finding his or her way to enlightenment by performing formalized seated meditation, this is not the case with Zen Buddhism. From the early Chinese schools of Ch'an forward, Zen has embraced the arts as a means for the practitioner to not only focus their individual meditative consciousness but also for the Zen master to expound their understanding of Nirvana to the world through various non-traditional means. Painting, poetry, gardening, the preparation of flowers, food, and drink, and the martial arts have are all viewed as effective means of meditation in Zen Buddhism.

The arts as an essential element of Zen Buddhism were initially influenced by the Taoist reverence for nature. From this reverence came a close alliance of the body and mind of the spiritualist with nature. As the centuries have progressed, the practitioners of Zen strive to become very consciously aware of the ever-moving patterns of nature. From this, they became interactive with this universal movement.

Zen Teachings in Art

From the artistic creations of Zen Buddhist masters, the viewer is presented with their unique concept of the essence of enlightenment. Each artistic portrayal delineates the universal understanding of communion with nature and the essential essence of human life in association with the Buddha-mind. From the presentation of Zen based art, the masters invoke inspiration in those who view these works. From this, they guide the practitioner down the pathway of Zen.

Zenga

Zen art is known in Japanese as, *"Zenga."* This term connotes the painting, and the calligraphy use to detail the various aspects of Zen Buddhism. Zenga uses black ink on white paper.

Whereas many styles of art, born from religion, use very exacting detail and elaborate coloration and brush strokes to create their religious works of art, this is not the case with Zenga. Zenga presents the true essence of art by the most simplistic and refined means possible.

Zenga is a means of focusing the mind of the painter to the degree where the individual self is lost and the true essence of the individual Buddha-mind is exposed. This is accomplished by representing an image, person, or natural scene in its most elemental form.

Zenga is a pathway of meditation. It is a method of bringing the artist into a natural state of contact with not only the inner-self but with the image that is being painted. For this reason, formality is left behind, exposing the true essence of art.

Historic Zenga

The early expression of Zenga first began to be witnessed during the sixth century in China. This art form began to flourish by the twelfth century in Japan. It was highly embraced as a meditative method by Zen monks of Japan's Edo period (1615-1868). One of the most prominent artists of this era was Hakuin Ekaku. Hakuin not only solidified Zenga as an essential element of Zen Buddhism but he helped to revitalize the, then faltering, Rinzai School of Zen.

Hakuin Ekaku

Hakuin Ekaku (1685-1768) is one of the elemental figures of mid-period Japanese Zen Buddhism. Hakuin was born in the village of Hara, near the base of Mount Fuji. He decided to become a Zen monk as a child. By the age of fifteen he had won the consent of his parents to embrace the monastic lifestyle. After many years of study, travel, and personal revelations, at the age of thirty-one he returned to his first temple, the Shoin-ji Temple, where he was installed as the abbot. At the age of forty-one Hakuin experienced the final stage of enlightenment while reading, *"The Lotus Sutra."* From that point forward, he spent the rest of his life leading other towards Nirvana.

Hakuin's mastery of Zen spread across the island nation of Japan. He was frequently asked to lecture at seminal Zen temples, and his writing were highly published and read. Hakuin did not begin painting until he was in his sixties, however. He continued the process until his death at eighty-four. As his years progressed, he turned to painting more and more as a means to portray his understanding of Zen. More than any other artists in Japanese history, the paintings of Hakuin have had a profound effect on the ongoing development of Zenga.

Calligraphy

The simple brush strokes of Zenga have proven to be an ideal tool to portray a Zen Masters understanding of enlightenment. In many cases a single word will be used in a Zenga paining. In other case, a Koan will be presented. As a tool of meditation, the students will not only seek the deeper meaning of the word, expression, or Koan, presented in the painting, but will also allow their mind to acutely focus on the presentation of the painted word or words. From this, the Zen practitioner achieves a focus for their meditation and is guided towards the Buddha-mind by the brush strokes of the artist.

Portraiture

One of the common subjects of Zenga is painting the portrait of legendary Buddhist figures such as Bodhidharma. Though no one knows what this historical figure actually looked like, through the century's interpretations of his image has filled many paintings. In these Portraitures the Zen artist attempts to tap into the essence of these historic figures and emulate their teachings by means of art.

Art as Meditation

Most school of traditional art train the student in methods in which they can paint the most mirror-like representation of an existing object. Even the abstract schools of art guide the students to represent their emotion or their interpretation of life in art. Zenga art does not follow this formula, however.

Zen understands that emotions are temporary. They are like the waves of the ocean—they arrive and then they retreat. Zen also understands this world is temporal. What is here today will not be here tomorrow. For this reason, attempting to grasp and hold onto a place or a moment in time only holds one bound to the illusions of this material world.

Moreover, most artists create their works of art from a space of ego. *This is my work, my style, my interpretation, my art.* Ego holds one bound to the thinking mind and to the thought of,

"I." If an individual is bound by thinking and the ego then they can never experience the essence of the Buddha-mind. For this reason, the Zenga artist strives to completely remove him or herself from the constraints of ego. They allow the art to be the art—not a personal creation, simply a method of focusing and aligning the physical mind with the Buddha-mind.

Zen is about spiritual freedom and enlightenment. It is not about personal creation. The Zen artist allows the creation to happen. They do not attempt to control, define, like or dislike. Like life, they simply allow their art to exist in its own perfection.

The Japanese Zen Tea Ceremony

As Zen Buddhism came to flourish in Japan, many aspects of Japanese culture came to embrace the simplicity and meditative mindset of Zen. This has been the case is all aspects of Japanese culture. In fact, Japanese culture cannot be separate from Zen, due to the fact that so much of the two have intermingled and come to formulate a single cohesive unit. This is the case with the Japanese Tea Ceremony.

Cha-no-yu

The Japanese term, *"Cha-no-yu"* literally translates as, *"Hot water for tea."* This term has come to define one of the most meditative aspects of drink preparation in recorded history. In fact, the proper preparation and presentation of the Tea Ceremony is understood to take years of practice before one has mastered the subtle realms of this technique.

The History of the Tea Ceremony

The drinking of tea is believed to have entered Japan via the hands of Chinese Buddhist monks in the ninth century. Tea soon became a widely embrace drink throughout the island nation.

During the ninth century the drinking of tea also become a Zen based formulized practice. Lu Yo (733-804), sometimes credited as being, *"The Sage of Tea,"* was the first to compose a text that details how one should properly plant, cultivate, harvest, prepare, and drink tea.

Lu Yo, as an abandoned child, spent his early years in a Chinese Buddhist monastery. Refusing to become a monk, as a teenage he escaped and became a traveling clown. He eventually settled in the Zhejiang region of China, where he became a master of the growth and preparation of tea. His writing traveled to Japan where they set the foundations for the Tea Ceremony to become a highly evolved practice.

By the sixteen century the Tea Ceremony had become a universally embraced revered practice in Japan. This formality was helped along by the Japanese tea master, Sen no Rikyu (1522–1591). He composed a poem that can be translated as, *"Without any spiritual training, you think you are drinking tea, but actually tea drinks you."* With this simple inspiration, the Tea Ceremony has continued to evolve throughout the centuries as both a practice based in Japanese culture and a meditative technique. The principals set forth in the Tea Ceremony are harmony, respect, purity, and tranquility.

In the Tea Ceremony all aspects of preparation, presentation, and consummation are view in the purest form. As such, the Tea Ceremony is considered one of the most revered forms of meditation in Japanese Zen Culture.

Zen and the Martial Arts

Certainly, Zen Buddhism has been one of the most essential elements in the development of the martial arts. This is especially the case with the Japanese martial arts; particularly the group of warriors that has become commonly referred to as, *"The Samurai."*

The title Samurai is a modern term. It was never used in ancient Japan to define a warrior. The word Samurai is based in the Japanese term *"Samurau."* The term came for the Heian period of Japanese history, which existed from 794 to 1185. *"Samurau,"* means to serve. The word, *"Samurai,"* therefore, connotes one who is in service to a master.

"Bushi," is the Japanese word that actually defined the formalized military warriors. Bushi, is the name given to those trained warriors who came

from families born from the warrior tradition. These families were known in Japanese as, *"Buke."*

The history of the Bushi goes back to the seventh century in Northern Japan. This formularized trend in Japanese culture occurred when families formed into clans to fight the invasive Ainu from modern day Sapporo, Japan. By the twelfth century the Bushi were a highly defined fighting class, who were not only battling the Honke, those of Nobel birth, for power over the island nation but additionally those warriors who were based in Buddhist temples, known as Sohei.

As the Buddhist religion came to extend over Japan, powerful Buddhist temples were substantiated. The temples came to be in possession of large amounts of farmland. The temple priests would lease the land and collect large taxes on its usage. The Sohei were the warriors who enforced the tax laws of the temple, as well as engaged in expansionistic battles against other Buddhist Monasteries.

The Japanese word, *"Gakusho,"* is the name for the upper hierarchy scholar priests. These priests generally drew lineage from one of the three Japanese Royal families. In addition, they controlled the Sohei and gained the spoils of Japanese Buddhist expansionism.

In the twelfth century the Minamoto family overthrew the other two reigning royal families:

the Fujiwara and the Taira. With their defeat, Minamoto no Yoritomo (1147-1199), established the first military government—historically referred to as a Kamakure Shogunate. This Shogunate led Japan into its Kamakura Period (1192-1333). This came to be the foundation for the historic period of Japanese history when the military class ruled the country.

Warfare as Meditation

As time progressed and military and Zen Buddhist hold substantiated itself over Japan, the Bushi progressively moved into a period where the techniques of the military arts became exercises in meditation. From this came the birth of the Ronin. The Japanese term, *"Ronin,"* literally translates as, *"Wave man,"* meaning that these warriors moved around and had no home. The Ronin were wandering warriors—not completely different from the Sadhu, *"Homeless monks"* of India, except in the fact that they were extensively trained in the art of warfare.

The Ronin were Zen based warriors, who, in association with Zen Priests, developed he martial arts of Japan to the level where expertise in warfare was not the only goal in becoming a skilled military technician. Instead, the art of war led to enlightenment.

Martial Arts as a Meditation

It is easily understood that the exacting style of movement training that the martial artist undergoes is an advanced form of movement meditation. The martial artist trains their body to move and react in ways never experienced by the average individual. Add to this the use of weapon, as was done with the ancient warriors of Japan, and an entirely new method of cohesive body-mind coordination is added to the meditation process.

Zen and the Way of the Sword

Between 1595 and 1598, after years of battle, the legendary Zen Buddhist warrior, Jinsuke Shigenobu (1546-1621), retreated to the Hikawa Temple to enter a period of austere meditation. During his stay he developed the meditative art of drawing the sword that he titled, *"Batto-jutsu."*

Jinsuke Shigenobu based his art upon the offensive and defensive techniques long used by samurai masters. He integrated the understanding of Yin and Yang—embrace the soft and the hard, into his newly defined system. What was born was a method where the sword practitioner, practicing alone, could focus his mind so precisely on the movement of the sword that he entered into a deep state of meditation. This art form laid the foundation for what is known in modern era as, *"Iaido."* Iaido is the meditative art of drawing the sword.

In the practice of Iaido the practitioner acutely focuses his consciousness on the art of removing the sword from its sheath and unleashing an offensive or defensive strike. In the practice of Iaido, no physical opponent is ever engaged in battle. This allows the mind of the practitioner to acutely focus on the meditative aspects of this art.

In the martial arts any weapon that is used is understood to be an extension of the body. The sword is witnessed not as an element onto itself. Instead, it is an elongation of the arm. With this understand, the sword becomes an integral part of the meditative process.

Shinmyoken

The Japanese term, *"Shinmyoken,"* is translated as *"Wondrous action of the soul of the sword."* This occurs when the mind is in perfect harmony with the body and the body perfectly unleashes the sword. From this focused consciousness the experience of drawing the sword is not witnessed as a physical activity. Instead, it is simply an action that occurs in accordance with the perfection of the universe. This is the state of action within non-action that the Zen Buddhist strives for when practicing any form of the martial arts.

Zen Buddhism and the Sword

The practitioner of Zen understands that each movement of life, whether it be physical or mental, must be performed with pure consciousness attached to it. From this comes a life lived in harmony.

With the conscious linking of the body and the mind, through highly advanced physical activities such as the martial arts, the individual mind is caused to focus intensely upon its actions. From this, the mind learns to possess acute focusing abilities. Therefore, from Iaido, or other forms of the martial arts, the Zen practitioner develops the ability to keep their mind focused upon, Pure thought, as opposed to the random roaming thoughts that are common in the mind of most individuals. With this, each action taken in association with the martial arts becomes a form of movement meditation. The practitioner of Zen may then take this understanding and apply it to all areas of their life, thereby making their every action a form of movement meditation.

PART IV
The Metaphysical Aspects
of Zen Buddhism

Zen Buddhism is a spiritual pathway of paradox and contradictions. Paradox and contradictions span the entire framework of Zen Buddhism. On one hand the techniques of Zen are very concrete—with a primary focus upon the need for formal seated meditation. On the other hand, it is understood that each person is already enlightened and no technique will ever actually lead a person to this ultimate end. Instead, each individual must simply remember and re-embrace the fact that they are already enlightened. For these reasons, Zen Buddhism is often referred to as, *"The pathless path."*

It must be understood that the discussion of Zen is not the practice of Zen. Innumerable words and been spoken and written about the subject of Zen. These discourses are designed to define Zen Buddhism to the degree that the mind of the average individual can come to comprehend the abstract fundamentals that form the foundation of this ancient understanding.

The ironic fact of Zen Buddhism is all Zen discourses are in exact contrast to the true essence of Zen. None-the-less, the analytical thinking mind must be provided with a set of criteria in which to guide itself towards the ultimately level of cosmic awareness. To this end, there are key ideologies that provide the Zen Buddhist practitioner with a pathway to embracing the experience of Nirvana.

Chapter 13

The Mind of No Mind

Throughout the evolution of Zen Buddhism, understandings have emerged that help to define this pathless path. From these detailed ideologies, the practitioner may come to more clearly understand what is expected and what may be encountered on this pathway of paradox.

Ku

"Ku," translated from Japanese means, *"Profound spiritual emptiness."* Ku is not an unconscious mental void. In fact, Ku is in complete contrast to any lack of awareness. Ku is a consciously encountered emptiness, achieved through acute mental focus. This conscious emptiness is the source point for the experience of Nirvana.

Ku is not a state of consciousness associated with the thinking mind. The mind of the average individual randomly travels from one thought onto the next and the next. Most people do not even choose to develop the ability to stop the thought process of their mind long enough to truly define why they are thinking what they are thinking, feeling what they are feeling, or experiencing what they are experiencing. Instead, they travel blindly through life, allowing something so temporary as a thought or an emotion to dominate their mind and the occurrences of their life experience.

Desires give birth to thoughts. Thoughts give birth to emotions. Emotions give birth to actions. Actions give rise to Karma. Karma is the law of cause and effect—as you sew so shall you reap. By consciously pursuing the understanding of Ku, Zen leads one away from the worldly path that ultimately culminates in the creation of Karma. Thus, the practitioner of Zen becomes free from the constraints of this worldly existence and is able to interact with the Buddha-mind.

Ku is a state of consciousness where the mind is no longer dominated by unnecessary thought patterns. In order for an individual to experience Ku, the foundation must be laid with the techniques designed to focus the mind. Ku may be achieved through the practice of Zazen. From Zazen the practitioner of Zen embraces the thoughtless mind, which is the essence of Ku.

Being and Non-Being

Zen accepts the existence of Being. Being is all that one sees, experiences, feels, and knows while the physical body binds one to this place we call life. Being is a human condition.

Zen also understands Non-Being. Non-Being can only be expressed in the state of Ku. Non-Being is present when the mind has been silenced and thoughts cease to exist.

Non-Being is not the thought of no-thought. The thought of no-thought is the illusion many people who meditate encountered when they train their mind to think that they are not thinking.

The practice of mantra meditation, taught in many schools of yoga, replaces the random thoughts of the practitioner with a single word or phrase. Though this style of meditation focuses the mind, it does not stop the mind from thinking. It simply replaces all thoughts with one thought. Though this style of meditation may be seen as beneficial, it does not lead to the essence of non-being.

Non-Being is at the heart of the paradox of Zen. Non-Being is defined by living in a human form but not being bound to the limitation of that human form. Again, this understanding presents the essence of Ku.

Sesshin

The Japanese word, *"Sesshin,"* means, *"The collecting of the mind."* Sesshin is commonly linked to the practice of Zazen.

Any physical or mental technique that focuses the mind can be used as a technique to achieve Sesshin. This is where the large difference between Zen Buddhism and the schools of Theravana Buddhism differ.

Zen embraces the necessity of all activity. No activity is more or less worthy than any other physical or mental activity. This remains true as long as the activity is performed consciously and is used as a method to focus the mind in order to encounter cosmic consciousness.

Mushin

The Japanese word, *"Mushin,"* means, *"Original Mind"* or *"No Mind."* Mushin witnesses a mind not bound by the desire for anything to be different than it currently is.

Mushin is a mindset that is not lost in judging life expereinces or in judging other people. For this reason, the individual who embraces Mushin is like a mirror reflecting the perfection of the world.

At the heart of Mushin is the acceptance that things in this universe are perfect. With no desire for things to be any different than they currently are, the individual who embraces Mushin exists in a state of constant acceptance. From this, they are not bound by the likes and dislikes of the common individual. Thus, they are able to interact with the enlightened Buddha-mind.

Ushin

Ushin is the opposite of Mushin. Ushin describes a mind fixated upon the temporary nature of this physical world. Ushin witnesses an individual believing that what he or she believes is the only right answer and that all other perceptions are incorrect. It also describes a person who is bound by desire. This is due to the fact that an individual with a mind fixated upon living and feeling a specific way is willing to do whatever it takes to maintain a specific lifestyle. From their actions, negative Karma is crated.

The mind locked in Ushin is based in ego and desire. It is argumentative and confrontational. As such, this person is constantly attracting unnecessary battles, both external and internal.

Mushin, on the other hand, is freedom. It allows an individual to pass from moment to moment with no confrontation. The individual who exists in a state of Mushin can blend in among all people and experience the true glory of an enlightened life.

Prajna

Prajna is the universal unmovable wisdom available to all people who seek its essence. Prajna is not unmovable in the sense of being stagnant, but unmovable in the firmness of a defined one-pointed wisdom.

Prajna is not a thought. Prajna is the instantaneousness of mastered action.

If the Zen Buddhist practitioner must contemplate his or her actions, then they are lost in the realms of the thinking mind, and they will never understand the spontaneousness that exists in the state of Prajna.

Prajna is evident when one lets go of individual ego. Individual ego is lost by coming to understand that your physical actions lead to nothing more than a movement in this transient place we call life. One's spiritual actions, on the hand, lead to enlightenment. Therefore, by letting go of personal self and embracing the enlightened Buddha-self, one is allowed to leave behind the constraints of the world and experience Nirvana.

Maya

"Maya," is the Sanskrit word for divine illusion. In Japanese this understanding is known as, *"Mayoi."*

The concept of Maya teaches us that all of life is an illusion. What we see, feel, and experience is not real. It is simply a projection of our own thinking mind.

This is where the perplexity of Maya is born, however. What is the thinking mind and how is it able to make us perceive a seemingly very-real reality if, in fact, it is all an illusion?

To the Westerner the concept of Maya is immediately dismissed as being an esoteric philosophy not based in empirical fact. To the practitioner of Zen Buddhism, however, this Western belief would immediately prove the existence of Maya; as the Western proof that there is a standard reality is based simply upon the consensus of unenlightened beings.

To come to understand the foundations for Maya it must be initially understood that everyone perceives this physical reality somewhat differently. This individual perception is based upon a person's own individual mindset that was formed by social, cultural, economic, educational, religious, and psychological events. This gives credence to the fact that there is no one absolute reality. The only reality is one that has been decided upon. Thus, physical reality is debatable.

The concept of Maya goes much deeper than this, however. It goes to the root of human consciousness and the basis of Zen Buddhist enlightenment.

Zen teaches us that each person is already enlightened. It is simply the veil of Maya that keeps us from recognizing this fact. Therefore, those who enter onto the path of Zen do so because they believe that they are separated from supreme consciousness. Thus, they begin the practices of Zen hoping that at some point they may finally remove the veil of Maya and reach enlightenment. This, however, is understood to be the ultimate example of Maya—that you must do something to reach enlightenment.

It must be understood that Nirvana is not based on a linear scale of higher and lower beings. Zen teaches that we all are already enlightened— some of us simply do not choose to realize and embrace this fact.

If you choose to embrace the essence of Zen and remember your original nature, you instantaneously achieve enlightenment. Though this may seem like a perplexing paradox, this paradox is the essence of Zen. And, to break through this veil of confusion, unleashed by Maya, is why people refine their mind through the practice of meditation and other Zen based techniques.

The ultimate illusion of Maya is that there is no illusion at all. We are all enlightened, we simply separate ourselves from this fact. Additionally, we are all locked in this physical form we call a body, which is a tool that we have been given in order to raise ourselves to clearer levels of mental, physical, and spiritual understanding.

Simply by embracing the paradoxical essence of Zen, all things fall into place and all things are understood. The veil of Maya is then lifted and in an instant this universe is understood, and the Buddha-mind is encountered.

PART V

Nirvana

Central to the core of Buddha's teachings is that enlightenment is the ultimate end-goal for all human beings. It is believed that those who choose to walk the path towards enlightenment are on the highest pathway of human existence and, therefore, are very consciously living their life—abandoning all actions that create negative Karma and are moving towards the Buddha-mind.

It is important to keep in mind, however, that the understanding of enlightenment did not originate with the Buddha. This understanding was in existence since the dawn of advancing human consciousness.

The Pali Canons of Buddhism recorded that there were twenty-eight Buddhas or enlightened beings that existed before Siddhartha Guatama. The number of those who have obtained this ultimate level of human consciousness has continued to multiply throughout the centuries.

Chapter 14

Nirvana: The Formalities

The Buddhist concept of to Nirvana arose from the ancient Hindu understanding of Samadhi. Samadhi, literally translated from the Sanskrit, means, *"Ecstasy."* Samadhi is the supreme level of human existence. In the Yoga sutras of the ancient Hindu sage Patangali, Samadhi defines the final step in human consciousness where the individual merges with the divine in a state of all-knowing self-realization and awareness.

There are three primary levels of Samadhi defined in the ancient scriptures. They are:

1. Savikalpa Samadhi
2. Nirvikalpa Samadhi
3. Sahaja Samadhi

Savikalpa Samadhi

Savikalpa Samadhi is the stage of enlightenment where the individual has focused his or her attention upon an image of the divine and has merged, becoming one with this deity or energy. At this level of enlightenment, a person is still aware of his or her human form. They are no longer, however, defined by personality or worldly desires.

In Hinduism the worship of a supreme deity is a very common form of spiritual practice. It is known as, *"Bhakti Yoga."* Throughout the centuries various schools of Buddhism have been known to practice a similar style of devotion—worshiping and praying to the Buddha. The Zen Buddhist does follow this path to spiritual realization, however. The Zen Buddhist understands that the Buddha reached the ultimate level of human consciousness. Once he had achieved this exalted state, he formalized a set of understandings and techniques that will cause those who practice them to become interactive with the same level of consciousness that he experienced. To this end, Savikalpa Samadhi, defines a style of enlightenment not saught after by the Zen Buddhist.

Nirvikalpa Samadhi

The second level of Samadhi is known as Nirvikalpa Samadhi. This level of enlightenment witnesses the individual devoid of self—all levels of bodily consciousness have been replaced by complete and total cosmic consciousness. This level of enlightenment is achieved when the Zen Buddhism has allowed his or her thinking mind to be forgotten. This may be achieved through meditation or other spiritual practices. With the thinking mind forgotten, the universal Buddha-mind is embraced.

Sahaja Samadhi

There is one final type of Samadhi. This is known as Sahaja Samadhi. This is instantaneous, total enlightenment. This is enlightenment that simply occurs in a moment of complete cosmic interaction.

It is understood in Zen Buddhism that there is no technique that can lead a person towards this level of supreme consciousness. Meditative techniques may train the mind to prepare it to recognize this level of Samadhi when it occurs, but this ultimate level of human consciousness can only be embraced when one completely lets go of self and merges with universal-self. For this, there is no technique, only complete mental and physical surrender.

The individual who achieves this level of Samadhi is known in Sanskrit as a *"Jivamukta," "The living liberated."* This is the style of Nirvana that the Buddha experienced and is the primary end-point that the Zen Buddhist walks towards.

Chapter 15

The Three Buddha

Throughout the centuries Buddhism has defined three types of people who obtain the ultimate stage of enlightenment, they are known as, *"The Three Buddhas."*

The Three Buddhas are:

1. Samyaksam Buddha
2. Pratyeka Buddha
3. Sravaka Buddha

Samyaksam Buddha

Samyaksam Buddha is one who reaches enlightenment through a path that was not laid before. What this means is that the Samyaksam Buddha does not follow a specific teacher and does not follow a set pattern of techniques that are defined by another religion or school of philosophic thought. Instead, the Samyaksam Buddha finds their own pathway to enlightenment and then spreads their message to others. Siddhartha Guatama, the Sakyamuni Buddha is known to be a Samyaksam Buddha.

Pratyeka Buddha

The Pratyeka Buddha is a silent Buddha. The Pratyeka Buddha is an individual who has obtained the ultimate stage of human consciousness by his own means, similar to a Samyaksam Buddha, yet does not go on a path of leading others to obtaining cosmic wisdom.

In the Mahayana tradition of Buddhism it is believed that only a very specific type of enlightened being possess the power to pass on the knowledge that leads another practitioner towards enlightenment. In fact, in some sects of Buddhism it is believes that a fully enlightened being can actually cause a person to obtain enlightenment. The Pratyeka Buddha, however, is defined as one who has reached personal enlightenment, but is not capable of transmitting that wisdom.

Sravaka Buddha

The Sravaka Buddha is one who has obtained Nirvana by hearing the Dharma and practicing it under the guidance of one who has obtained enlightenment. Due to the fact that the Sravaka Buddha has been schooled in all aspects of the mystic path to enlightenment, they are understood to possess the ability to teach others and guide them toward their own enlightenment.

Chapter 16

Understanding Enlightenment

Central to the core of Zen Buddhism is the accepted understanding that we <u>all</u> are already enlightened. We each simply need to remember this fact. It is further understood that it is the thinking mind of the individual that keeps him or her from embracing this self-realization. It also part of the essential teaching of Zen Buddhism, however, that one cannot simply desire enlightenment. For if one has any desire for enlightenment, enlightenment will never be experienced. This is due to the fact that desire sets one apart from enlightenment. It is at this point that we encounter one of the supreme paradoxes of Zen Buddhism, *"The ultimate goal of Zen is enlightenment. Yet, if you seek enlightenment, it can never be found."*

This is where all of the techniques of Zen Buddhism find their basis—as a means to shake the practitioner loose from their thinking mind in order to make them embrace the non-thinking mind in order to remove themselves from desire, in order to loose all thought, in order to achieve Nirvana.

This is why Zen is abstract to the masses, yet understandable for those who have cleansed their mind of desire and dwell within a true to space of ethereal silence. In this place, the Zen understanding of, *"No-desire within desire is understood."*

Embracing Nirvana

Since the dawn of humanity there has been the concept of less and more. As human history as evolved, those who have raised themselves to the top of culture have been believed to be worthy of veneration. This is especially the case on the spiritual path. One who has obtained enlightenment is considered the highest and most holy. At the pinnacle of enlightened beings is that of Siddhartha Guatama, The Sakyamuni Buddha. The Buddha symbolizes all that is pure, above reproach, and at the top of the ultimate level of human existence.

We can look to the earliest Sanskrit and Pali writings and read about this exalted being and his teaching. But these writing are simply representations about this man who transcended material understanding and laid a path to higher consciousness that has been followed for centuries. Those who lived after him documented the actual realizations of the Buddha and his experiences. From this style of historic legacy, legend has been born. And though legend is glorious and beautiful, legend is only legend. What the Buddha actually experienced and taught is lost forever.

This being understood, you can begin to reformulate your concept of Nirvana with a clearer perception of how it affects you—for no longer must you base your definition of Nirvana solely upon its most exalted proponent.

Satori

The word, *"Satori,"* describes the state of instantaneous enlightenment. It is understood in Zen Buddhism that no matter how long one walks upon the spiritual path, enlightenment happens in an instant and flashes of this supreme consciousness can be invoked from virtually anything: a Koan, reading a spiritual text, watching a bird fly through the air, or the slap of a bamboo shaft from the Roshi when an individual has fallen asleep during Zazen.

The Zen Buddhist practitioner prepares him or herself for this instantaneous enlightenment and willingly accepts it when it appears.

Walking the Path to Enlightenment

Walking the path to enlightenment begins from an untold number of motivating factors. Once on this path, however, a spiritual teacher, several teachers, or the philosophic belief may guide you. As you progress along the mystical road of Zen, you will come to realize that all of the formalities you initially held onto, your religion, your teacher, your practices, and even your own image of self begin to fall away. What remains is a pure being that is no longer bound by the traditional desires and rationales of the material world.

Nirvana Now

Throughout history the pathway to enlightenment has been confounded by definitions and dogma set forth from an untold number of sources. This ideally illustrates the paradoxical essence of Zen that causes the practitioner to move beyond the known, the accepted, and the understood—ultimately entering into a state of All-Knowingness. But, if teachings and dogma will not get you there, how does one travel the path to Nirvana?

Nirvana is the end result of the practice of Zen. The paradoxical problem that exists in this mentality is that as long as you set your sights on a goal, be it a new house, a new car, a new job, a new lover, or enlightenment, you are bound to the constraints of material existence by that desire. And, desire itself, no matter how seemingly holy, keeps you from self-realization and cosmic consciousness. Therefore, practice Zen, seek nothing but what comes naturally from each step, and you will not be restrained by the controlling hands of desire. Thus, you will be free and wholly on your pathway to enlightenment.

Nirvana has been defined as the ultimate step of human consciousness and evolution. For centuries, religions and spiritual teachers have defined the steps one must progress through to reach this final level of human understanding. The problem is, those who have defined the steps to enlightenment are, for the most part, admittedly unenlightened. How does an individual who is not enlightened, teach you how to become enlightened?

Many teachers on the Zen Buddhist pathway continually separate themselves from their own enlightenment by stating, *"An enlightened teacher would say..."* But, by believing that somebody else, *"Knows,"* and they do not, they continually block the possibility of encountering this most natural state of human existence. They obviously do not understand the most essential teaching of Zen, *"That we all are enlightened."*

Enlightenment is not a rank that is earned. Monkhood is a rank. Priesthood is a rank. But, enlightenment is not a rank.

In each of us, enlightenment already exists. The majority of us have simply forgotten this very obvious truth. Zen reminds us of what we have forgotten.

The plight of many practitioners and teachers alike, is that they falsely believe that enlightenment is something off in the distance and not obtainable. That one must practice several lifetimes of austerities to ever touch its realms.

This common misnomer is the exact thing that keeps so many people from encountering Nirvana—their belief that it is a thing that exists somewhere off in the distance. This is incorrect. Zen teaches us that enlightenment is right here, right now. By letting go of the known, you immediately encounter it.

Why then, do so many people live in caves for years, sit in Zazen for hour after hour, and perform all kinds of seemingly insane forms of austerities to encounter Nirvana? This is the ultimate illusion of Zen, that you must do something to obtain Nirvana.

Nirvana is not about doing. Nirvana is about undoing. As long as you hold yourself to the belief that you are not worthy of obtaining enlightenment—you must perform some task, overcome some karmic obstacle to obtain Nirvana, Nirvana can never be known. So many teachers who have devoted their lives to the process of enlightenment have proved this. They have taught what they have learned from others. They have quoted the scriptures. They have lived a good life and have helped others. What they have not done, however, is to let go of the illusion that they are not enlightened.

Let go of the thoughts that you are not pure enough, holy enough, or of a high enough incarnation to embrace Nirvana and it will come rushing towards you. The ultimate Zen Buddhist teaching is that, *"The only thing keeping you from Nirvana is you."* Move forward and embrace your own Nirvana.

Glossary

Akimcanya Ayatana: The experience of spiritual nothingness.

Arada Kalama: Guru of the Buddha.

Arhat: Disciples of the Buddha.

Asana: Physical posture.

Ashoka: Ancient Buddhist king.

Bodhidharma: Indian Buddhist sage credited with laying the foundation of Zen.

Bodh Gaya: The location where Buddha was enlightened.

Bushi: Japanese warrior.

Ch'an: The Chinese predecessor to Zen.

Chaung Tzu: Ancient Taoist sage.

Daruma: Japanese name for Bodhidharma.

Dharma: The way.

Diamond Sutra: Mahayana Buddhist text.

Dogen: (1200-1253) Buddhist sage, founder of the Soto School of Zen.

Eisai: (1141-1215) Buddhist sage, founder of the Rinzai School of Zen.

Fudo no Shisei: Immovable Posture.

Fushiro: Without thinking.

Gakusho: Buddhist temple landholders of Japan.

Guru: Spiritual teacher.

Hakuin Ekaku: (1685-1768) Japanese Buddhist sage.

Hara: The bodies center point.

Hishiryo: Thought without thought.

Hokkaijo: Hands in perfect balance with the universe.

Hui-ko: Chinese Buddhist sage.

Hui-neng: (637-713) Chinese Buddhist sage.

Hung-jen: (601-674) Chinese Buddhist sage.

Hwa Rang: Ancient Korean Buddhist warriors.

Hyang-ga: Native songs of Korea.

Iaido: Japanese art of drawing the sword.

Karma: The law of cause and effect.

Kinhin: Walking meditation.

Kung Fu Tzu: Confucius. Ancient Taoist sage.

Koan: Zen statement used to invoke enlightenment.

Lao Tzu: Ancient Taoist sage.

Mahasanghika: One of the first schools to divide the Buddhist religion.

Mahayana: One of the two primary schools of Buddhism.

Maiterya: The unborn Buddha.

Mudra: Formation of the hands.

Munen Mushin: The spiritual state of emptiness.

Mushin: Original or No Mind.

Naiva Samjna Asamjna Ayatana: The experience of conscious unconsciousness.

Nihonshoki: Japanese Buddhist text.

Nirvana: Enlightenment.

Padma Asana: Full lotus seated posture.

Pali Canon: Ancient Buddhist manuscript.

Prajna: Universal unmovable wisdom.

Prajnaparamita Sutra: Mahayana Buddhist text.

Ronin: Wandering samurai warriors.

Roshi: Teacher.

Sadhana: Spiritual practice.

Sadhu: Homeless holy men of India.

Sakyamuni Buddha: Buddha from the Kingdom of Sakya.

Samadhi: Enlightenment.

Sanga: The Spiritual Brotherhood.

Seiza: Kneeling posture.

Sesshin: Collecting of the mind.

Seng-ts'an: Chinese Buddhist sage.

Shiryo: Thinking.

Sramana: Ancient group of East Indian holy men.

Satori: Instantaneous enlightenment.

Shikantaza: Japanese, *"Just sitting."*

Shoshang: The Shaolin Monastery where Bodhidharma taught.

Siddhartha Guatama: Birth name of the Buddha.

Sohei: Buddhist samurai warriors of Japan.

Sthavarivada: One of the first schools to divide the Buddhist religion.

Tao-hsui (580-651): Ancient Chinese Buddhist sage.

Ta Mu: Chinese name for Bodhidharma.

Tanden: The burning place of energy – the Hara.

Tao Te Ching: Ancient Taoist text.

The Inner Chapters: Ancient Taoist text.

Theravada: One of the two primary traditions of Buddhism.

Udraka Ramaputra: Guru of the Buddha.

Ushin: mind fixated on the physical world.

Vibhajyavada: Self Analysis.

Vinaya: The Buddhist Code of Conduct.
Zendo: School of Zen.
Zenga: Zen art.

Recommended Reading

An, Thich Thien, Zen Philosophy, Zen Practice. New York, Dharma Publishing, 1975.

Bodhidharma, Broughton, Jeffrey L. The Bodhidharma Anthology: The Earliest Records of Zen. Berkeley, University of California Press, 1999.

Conze, Edward. Buddhist Wisdom: The Diamond Sutra and The Heart Sutra. New York, Vintage, 2001.

Dogen. Beyond Thinking: A Guide to Zen Meditation. Boston, Shambhala, 2004.

Dogen, Beyond Thinking: A Guide to Zen Meditation. Boston, Shambhala, 2004

Dogen, Eihei, Tanahashi, Kazuaki, Ed. Moon in a Dewdrop: Writings of Zen Master Dogen. New York, North Point Press, 1995.

Dumoulin, Heinrich, Heisig, James W., Knitter, Paul F. Zen Buddhism: A History. New York, MacMillan Publishing Company, 1988.

Hanh, Thich Nhat, Levitt, Peter, The Heart of Understanding: Commentaries on the Prajnaparamita Heart Sutra. Berkeley, Parallax Press, 1988.

Huikai, Cleary, Thomas, Trans., Unlocking the Zen Koan: A New Translation of the Zen Classic Wumenguan. Berkeley, North Atlantic Books, 1997.

Ikeda, Daisaku, Endo, Takanori, The Wisdom Of The Lotus Sutra. Santa Monica, World Tribune Press, 2000.

Kapleau, Philip, The Three Pillars of Zen: Teaching, Practice, and Enlightenment. New York, Anchor, 1989.

Kato, Bunno, Threefold Lotus Sutra. Tokyo, Kosei Publishing Company, 1989.

Lee, O-Young, In This Earth and In That Wind: This is Korea. Seoul, Royal Asiatic Society, 1983.

Leighton, Taigen Dan, Dogen's Extensive Record : A Translation of the Eihei Koroku. Somerville, Dharma Publications, 2004.

Miura, Isshu, Miura, Sasaki, Ruth, The Zen Koan: Its History and Use in Rinzai Zen. New York, Harvest/HBJ Book, 1984.

Mizuno, Kogen, Buddhist Sutras: Origin, Development, Transmission. Tokyo, Kosei Publishing Company, 1982.

Mizuno, Kogen, Essentials of Buddhism: Basic Terminology and Concepts of Buddhist Philosophy and Practice. Boston, Tuttle Publishing, 1997.

Nanomli, Bhikku, The Middle Length Discourses of the Buddha, Somerville, Wisdom Publications, 1989.

Nyogen, Senzaki, The Iron Flute: 100 Zen Koans. Boston, Tuttle Publishing, 2000.

Reat, Noble Ross, Buddhism: A History. Jain Publishing Company, London, 1996.

Sekida, Katsuki, Zen Training: Methods and Philosophy. Boston, Weatherhill, 1975.

Senzaki, Nyogen, The Iron Flute: 100 Zen Koans. Boston, Tuttle Publishing, 2000.

Sunim, Kusan, The Way of Korean Zen. New York, Weatherhill, 1985.

Suzuki, Daisetz Teitaro, Zen Buddhism. New York, Image, 1996.

Suzuki, Daisetz Teitaro, Zen and Japanese Culture. Princeton, Princeton University Press, 1970.

Suzuki, Daisetz Teitaro, The Awakening of Zen. Boston, Shambhala, 2000.

Suzuki, Daisetz Teitaro, Lankavatara Sutra. Boston, Shambhala, 1978.

Suzuki, Daisetz Teitaro, Studies in Zen. New York, E. P. Dutton, 1963.

Suzuki, Daisetz Teitaro, Living by Zen: A Synthesis of the Historical and Practical Aspects of Zen Buddhism. Boston, Weiser Books, 1972.

Suzuki, Daisetz Teitaro, An Introduction to Zen Buddhism. New York, Grove/Atlantic, 1991.

Suzuki, Daisetz Teitaro, Manual of Zen Buddhism. New York, Grove Press, 1960.)

Suzuki, Shunryu, Not Always So : Practicing the True Spirit of Zen. New York, Perennial, 2003

Suzuki, Shunryu, Branching Streams Flow in the Darkness: Zen Talks on the Sandokai. Berkeley, University of California Press, 2001.

Tamura, Yoshiro, Hunter, Jeffrey, Japanese Buddhism: A Cultural History. Tokyo, Kosei Publishing Company, 2001.

Thien-An, Thich, <u>Zen Philosophy, Zen Practice</u>. Berkeley, Dharma Publishing, 1975.

Uchiyama, Kosho, <u>Opening the Hand of Thought: Foundations of Zen Buddhist Practice</u>. Somerville, Wisdom Publications, 2004.

Vimalakirtinirdesa, <u>The Holy Teaching of Vimalakirti: A Mahayana Scripture.</u> Philadelphia, Pennsylvania State University Press, 1987.

Waddell, Norman, <u>Essential Teachings of Zen Master Hakuin.</u> Boston, Shambhala, 1994.

Waddell, Norman, <u>Zen Words for the Heart: Hakuin's Commentary on the Heart Sutra.</u> Boston, Shambhala, 1996.

Watson, Burton, Trans., <u>The Lotus Sutra.</u> New York, Columbia University Press, 1993.

Watts, Alan, W., <u>The Way of Zen.</u> New York, Vintage, 1999.

Yamada, Koun, <u>Gateless Gate : The Classic Book of Zen Koans</u>. Somerville, Wisdom Publications, 2004.

About the Author

Scott Shaw is a prolific author and filmmaker. He is recognized as one of the preeminent Martial Arts Masters of the Western world and is at the forefront of integrating spirituality into the Martial Arts. During his youth he became deeply involved with Eastern Meditative Thought. This guided him to Asia where he has been initiated into Buddhist, Hindu, and Sufi sects. Today, Shaw frequently returns to Asia, documenting obscure aspects of Asian culture in words and on film. He is a frequently featured contributor to Martial and Meditative Art journals and is the author of numerous books on Zen Buddhism, Yoga, Meditation, Asian Studies, Ki Science, and the Martial Arts.

www.ingramcontent.com/pod-product-compliance
Lightning Source LLC
Chambersburg PA
CBHW070800100426
42742CB00012B/2207